The
Complete

M1 GARAND

Dedicated to Lyman Pollock, who first told me and taught me about the M1 Garand and an ugly winter in a Belgian town called Bastogne.

The Complete

M1 GARAND

A Guide for the Shooter and Collector

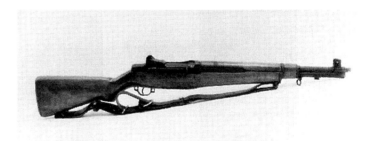

Jim Thompson

PALADIN PRESS
BOULDER, COLORADO

Also by Jim Thompson:
The Classic M1 Garand: An Ongoing Legacy for Shooters and Collectors

The Complete M1 Garand: A Guide for the Shooter and Collector
by Jim Thompson

Copyright © 1998 by Jim Thompson

ISBN 13: 978-0-87364-984-1
Printed in the United States of America

Published by Paladin Press, a division of
Paladin Enterprises, Inc.
Gunbarrel Tech Center
7077 Winchester Circle
Boulder, Colorado 80301 USA
+1.303.443.7250

Direct inquiries and/or orders to the above address.

PALADIN, PALADIN PRESS, and the "horse head" design
are trademarks belonging to Paladin Enterprises and
registered in United States Patent and Trademark Office.

Visit our Web site at www.paladin-press.com

CONTENTS

WARNING

Technical data presented here, particularly data on ammunition and on the use, adjustment, and alteration of firearms, inevitably reflects the author's individual beliefs and experience with particular firearms, equipment, and components under specific circumstances that the reader cannot duplicate exactly. The information in this book should therefore be used for guidance only and approached with great caution. Neither the author nor the publisher assumes any responsibility for the use or misuse of information contained in this book.

PREFACE

No American battle rifle boasts the distinguished and victorious reputation the M1 Garand earned in nearly 40 years' service. From the seriously flawed and controversial "gas trap" guns of 1936 and four years of failure, the 1940-41 and subsequent "gas port" guns and their many revisions were built in the United States until at least 1956 as military rifles, delivered from Italy until at least the late 1960s, and, until recently, made in a nonspecification, cast form by a couple of stateside firms. The service rifle outperformed the venerable '03 Springfield and all variants thereof in competition, shooting scores as early as 1946 with service ammunition that the ancient boltgun never equaled with prewar match loads.

Until recently, M1 was somewhat uncommon in civilian hands. Galef in New York had released a few lend-lease returnees as early as 1946. Driblets were released from military inventory via the NRA-affiliated Department of Civilian Marksmanship until that program was briefly frozen, and then again when it was reopened (and it will likely soon close again, this time probably marking the demise of the DCM itself).[1] In the mid-1960s, some welded-up demilitarized rifles got onto the market along with small shipments of "reimports"—rifles sold outright for cash to foreign governments and released back here

---

1. What used to be the U.S. Army's DCM (Department of Civilian Marksmanship) has been dissolved, replaced by what is basically a private corporation called the CMP (Civilian Marksmanship Program). Under that umbrella, M1s may go up in price as high as $400 or higher but will continue to be available. Various auctions, etc., and programs for other firearms may be instituted. The various freezes in the program(s) appear to be over, though it is now more important than ever for the Garand buff to keep a close watch on the system.

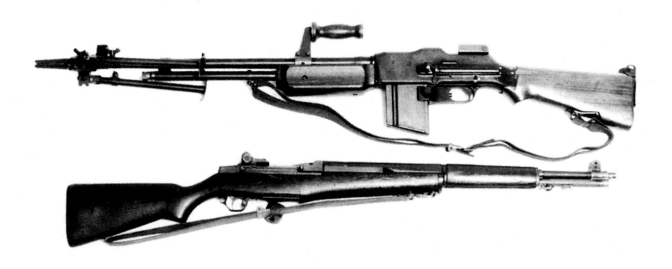

PHOTO 1. Launched by bloody lessons learned in "The War to End All Wars," massive efforts to increase the independence, versatility, and firepower of small American infantry units were championed by radicals in the Roosevelt administration. This meant vastly better communications; more mobility—some wheeled, some tracked; and a fast-firing rifle that was the core of the fire team and the squad, with all other small arms acting as support. The B.A.R. (a World War I veteran that saw some actual combat at the very end) and the M1 Garand proved to be the very guts of the weapons end of this approach, which was fought tooth and nail by traditionalists in the military and was the antithesis of the European approach. This pair—the M.1918A2 B.A.R. on top and the M1 on the bottom—was made by Winchester, and both rifles were delivered at the very end of World War II.

as surplus. This latter group comprises some of the best M1s ever to hit the stateside market from a collector's point of view, for it stands the very least chance of having seen extensive, repeated rebuilds. Since 1985, vast quantities of Garands have entered the United States from Italy, Morocco, China, Korea, and elsewhere.

This book primarily concerns the practical M1 from both collecting and shooting points of view. If you own a Garand, something herein will benefit you, if only the accompanying compendium of suppliers or the troubleshooting guide. Collectors may find Part IV more interesting than the main text, especially if they do not shoot.

It is my intention to offer the practical information in a greatly condensed form, stripped of a great deal of the verbiage and obsolete misinformation dispensed concerning the Garand, for example:

1. Seventh round stoppage. Not a myth, though it only ever truly applied to about the first 52,000 or so rifles (basically all the

unmodified "gas traps" and several thousand of the early "gas port" rifles). The defect resulted from a potpourri of missed specifications and stresses. But the hang-ups were quickly addressed and the underlying problems solved, and, save for a tiny quantity of rifles that somehow escaped corrective rebuilds and welding work, no such rifles should exist today. Anyone who relays this tale either has an extremely rare rifle or a very vivid imagination.

2. The "DCM Rifle as Virgin" myth. M1s were subjected to vast and irregular rebuilds and refinishes. I have seen precious few "original" DCM M1s, and I have never seen a DCM Winchester with anything close to original finish (generally, the Winchester markings are nearly gone). DCM guns—though there are surely exceptions, especially among the recently auctioned rifles—are generally the *most heavily modified of all*. Most have seen many refinishes. Most do have good barrels and are at least safe. But the myth of the "pedigreed," "virginal," or "original" DCM M1 is less truthful than the unicorn stories of old.

3. The myth of the magic brand(s). This one's fascinating, if only because reality is almost a reverse image of "common knowledge," and no single fiction about this rifle more clearly illustrates how insane rumors, misinformation, and disinformation grow and circulate.

The photos are intended to be closer, larger, and more detailed than commonly seen. Most of the guns here come from Arlington Ordnance, not because they're the best—though in many cases, they were—but because Arlington Ordnance was the only supplier who could furnish me with what I needed. (For the curious, I owned most of the rifles pictured here, though by the time you read this the financial outlay and long, long time delay in actually getting this project published will more or less guarantee that I will have sold all my rifles. This book cost me a great deal of money, in terms of rifles, ammunition, and photography.)

If parts of this book seem radical, controversial, or blasphemous, I'm pleased. I did my research with the rifles themselves and hard-working armorers and smiths, with no input from vested interests and no subsidies from anyone. Technical operations orders were digested, what few documents I could access recorded, and many times gems for analysis or photography showed up from unexpected sources. We military collectors are regarded as riffraff by many other collectors and by much of the "highbrow" end of the shooting community—even more so by those in government. And by the way, don't buy into the cheap hype—pressure on us comes from both sides of the political spectrum, and any party that finds a new buzzword handy will try to victimize us. It seems very difficult for much of the world to understand that smelly old military rifles (at least in that respect critics are right, for cosmolined Garands do truly smell foul) can be at once a lot of fun and a scholarly pursuit. But, of course, this has all gone on since some cave man hung up a favorite stone axe and began boasting how strong and how many the saber-toothed tigers slain. And then, just as now, I'm sure all the sizes and numbers grew with each retelling.

The Garand, though, really was in those important fights and for years was truly unique and uniquely effective.

THE M1 GARAND: AN OVERVIEW AND HISTORY

Those who jot down the production life of John Garand's rifle as if it were a continuous span from 1936 to 1957 are not wrong but should add, at least parenthetically, that the original 1936 machine was basically a failed prototype. Most of the first batches of rifles, built exclusively at Springfield Armory, were welded up as/where required, reconfigured with new barrels and gas cylinders, and returned to service. Very few exist intact, though there is a surprising supply of early parts, many unused.

In the course of this book, the term "Model 1936" may turn up, but the term was never official. It refers to the first few thousand gas trap rifles and may refer to gas trap guns generically. To the military, they were all M1s, and subtypes exist only in relationship to specific parts.

The breakdown of manufacturers and rifles that follows is a primer for the rest of this book and its specialized parts and subsections.

To shooters, there is no "magic" to any particular manufacturer. Usually inaccuracy of the Garand involves something that is worn out, loose, or misinstalled—or, of course, a lousy shooter. Sloppy bedding, loose gas cylinders, tired barrels, lousy ammo . . . these are usually the causes. Only a very few parts are chronic problems, and this book will try to discern them all.

This book won't detail every marking on the Garand, though the photos should be helpful in gaining familiarity with the system. One should make some notations, however, to help determine the age of some parts and thus analyze a rifle's history. The maker's codes are very simply figured and are literal: "SA" = Springfield Armory, U.S. (Springfield, MA); "WRA" = Winchester Repeating Arms; "SAI" or "SA" with ® to denote trademark = Springfield Armory, Incorporated (Springfield, IL, private firm); "IHC" = International Harvester; "HRA" = Harrington and

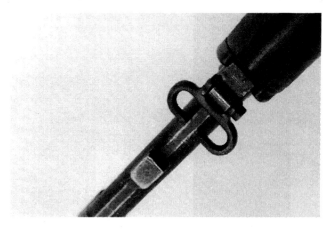

PHOTO 2. Virtually none of the mysterious letters on the gas cylinders of virtually all vintages of Garand from virtually all sources have been deciphered. Usually single letters, they were largely finish codes, used in a frantic effort to determine how best to make the stainless steel of the cylinder nonreflective. Acids, phosphates, plating techniques, and even paints were tried to increase permanence and darkness of the patina, and none seemed to work very well.

PHOTO 3. Three M1 operating rods: (top) -6 uncut, (middle) postwar replacement D 35382, and (bottom) "77" series National Match. Note stress crack and dislodged material at corner of bolt detent on the top unit, suggesting that this rod will soon fail and/or separate. The -6 rod does not belong on a rifle that is being fired.

PHOTO 4. The swept-back "knuckle" of this operating rod marks it as a very early style or a Winchester. This style was out of production at Springfield by mid-1940, but Winchester never adopted the changes to strengthen and modernize this part until after the end of the war, with the WIN-13 series. This one carries the hemispherical relief cut added on rebuilds after the war.

PHOTO 5. Stainless steel pistons of typical M1 Garand operating rods. Note the thicker stock of the bottom unit, a "77" series. Note also pitting and erosion on the top unit, which has been repistoned, but which obviously saw extensive prior use with corrosive ammunition and was not properly cleaned. All three are usable.

Richardson; "PB" = Pietro Beretta; "BMB" = Breda (Beretta) Maschina Brescia, sometimes accompanied by subcodes to identify subfactories. While these are the major codes, ultimately hundreds of contractors produced parts and assemblies for the M1 program, and you'll find "RA" on operating rods, "SuS" (Sauer and Sohn) on some German-made replacement parts, and "LMR" on original International Harvester barrels. To the collector, some advice: on Springfield guns, almost everything comes from Springfield, but on all others, do not panic if a small letter or number code doesn't jive with the pattern of the rest of the rifle (see the photo sections for some details). There were hundreds of small subcontractors, such that "A" and "CM" appear on many wartime Winchester and even some Springfield guns, and collectors argue considerably over which tiny part is "correct" for a particular rifle.

Knowing the parts number code can save the unwary from a financial or medical disaster, such as paying a high price for a rewelded demilitarized receiver or, worse, suffering an injury as a result of a high-speed operating rod separation—chronic to the old, uncut World War II and earlier original rods but ordered off all rifles as early as 1946 (see the illustrations relating to operating rods). These rods can be worth $100 or more to collectors, but shooters do not need or want them.

Somewhere in the parts number stamped on most major and some minor Garand parts is a five-digit core identification number. On the operating rod, for example, it's 35382, usually prefixed by a "D" for "drawing number," followed by suffixes to identify modifications. Don't memorize the system. The very first operating rods often bore no number at all. But the easiest identified "first model" is D 35382-0, sometimes overstamped and modified much later. Wartime rods ran to D 35382-9, with some small number of higher suffixed experimentals. First-generation postwar replacements, with cutout, were marked D 35382. First postwar production used a modified but still easily identifiable part number, prefixing the core number with "65" and using the maker's code as a suffix, such as in 6535382 SA.

The very latest (and, from the shooter's point of view, best and least likely to be worn out) parts were made after the rifle was out of production, often prefixed 77, as in the last Springfield operating rods. However, the rod was made sturdier and different welding techniques were used on these lots, so the final number became 77 90722. These were made well into the 1960s and perhaps into the 1970s. These distinctions are vital with some parts, such as when a Winchester receiver is encountered bearing the postwar receiver code up front right (e.g., 65 28291 3C SA, which tells one it's a postwar Springfield receiver up front, welded to a sought-after and fairly rare Winchester rear—or, in other words, a welded up demil/remil ca. 1960-64, and at the very bottom of the barrel in terms of dollar value). When the base part number changes, the part has been changed in a major way; prefix alterations (you'll see many specific applications in the photo

PHOTO 6. Easily identified Garand "business ends," obvious by the sight, gas cylinder lock, and gas cylinder lock plug configurations. From left: postwar, late war, and early World War II. Details will be found in the following chapters and subchapters.

PHOTO 7. Early WRA M1 with Winchester-marked ammunition and World War II Winchester ad. Note that, for shooting convenience, this original Winchester rifle bears a late "National Match" rear sight aperture.

and detail sections of this book) simply reflect later production indexed by a different drawing page number. However, as with a good reading of the rules before sitting down to play poker with strangers, forewarned is forearmed. The "D" letter for "drawing" was ultimately deleted on many parts. In fact, generally, as time wore on, fewer parts were numbered at all, and by the end of World War II, only more expensive parts bore numbers.

THE RIFLES BY MANUFACTURER

Springfield Armory ("SA" code). Manufactured from 1936-40 and 1940-56, with very few produced between late 1945 and early 1950. Some National Match rifles were delivered long after 1956. Springfield was the original M1 manufacturer; it built more than anyone, especially during World War II, and, depending on serial number ranges, generally evinced any and all changes first. World War II guns are most common, but there's absolutely nothing wrong with them unless some actual damage has occurred. Postwar

PHOTOS 8-11.   All the M1's contemporary "competitors"—full-power semiautos—evinced enough production or service glitches that they never saw extensive service in the field with ordinary infantry. They are, from top to bottom: [8] German G.41W, [9] German G.43/K.43, [10] Soviet Tokarev M40, and [11] U.S. Johnson M.1941.

PHOTO 12. Postwar .30/06 Springfield Armory, Incorporated barrels were marked with caliber and "Geneseo, Illinois." This one has been marked by the installing smith with full data, similar to a military designation, including the date the tube was installed. These barrels were excellent shooters. This is the match version, installed on a ca.1956 receiver.

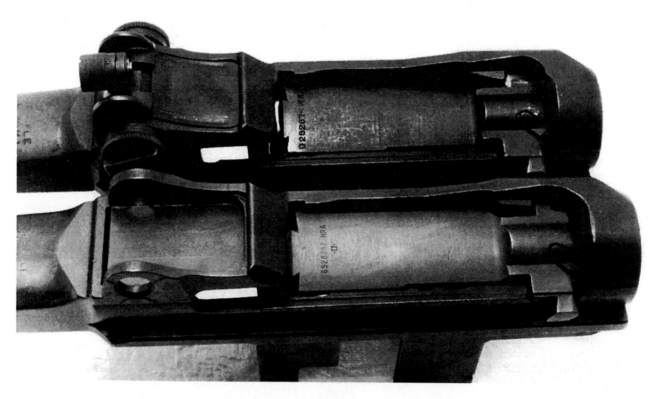

PHOTO 13. Virtually everything on the Garand changed during its long production life. The upper receiver in this photo is the crude, primitive Winchester -2 series; the lower a late H&R, numbered well over 5 million. The Winchester has been fitted with a National Match sight aperture in preparation for actual shooting, though the sight was not introduced until 20 years after this receiver was delivered (this is a convenience for shooters). Note the many detail and contour changes near the chamber area and the much heftier "horseshoe" area aft of the rear sight fitting on the postwar receiver. Most Winchester receivers and virtually all the bolts were out of true (basically out of specification). Not until the postwar 'WIN-13 series (ordered during the war but delivered after contracts had expired), whose serial numbers overlap 1.6 million Springfields, did Winchester evince the willingness or capability to update its production by incorporating improvements. Later receivers are stronger and, obviously, tend to be less worn.

Springfields of the last receiver variant are superb and those numbered over 6,000,000 quite rare.

All permutations of gray to greenish gray and black or charcoal will be found on Springfield guns, but most were very dark gray to black when issued. The medium gray found on most extant guns is a fairly certain sign the gun has been refinished. Many different materials were used on the M1, and finish specifications were different for various parts. It is fairly accurate to say that a "virginal" Springfield M1 should not be absolutely uniform in finish color. Springfield Armory experimented with many finishes late in the rifle's career, particularly on gas cylinders, and a few seemingly original rifles seem to have been oxided or black chrome plated at the armory.

Winchester Repeating Arms ("WRA" code). Manufactured in World War II only. Most Winchester Garand receivers are of the early 1940 -2 (dash two) configuration. Only the WIN-13 receivers, whose numbers overlap various Springfield contracts, showed any of the 32 major changes instituted at Springfield Armory during the war, as Winchester proved unwilling or unable to change its production line. Virtually all Winchester receivers were finished black/charcoal, though other parts may be various colors. Metal work on ancillary surfaces of Winchester M1s is quite rough, more so than on any other M1s, and many parts were marked in a nonregulation or very early manner. Wartime Winchester barrels were not customarily dated. Parts numbers are generally applied as on 1940 vintage specifications.

Springfield Armory Inc., Geneseo, IL ("SAI" code; note ® under logo). These are all postwar rifles, produced on investment cast receivers rather than specification forgings. As of this writing, new receivers are no longer being produced. Springfield began production in the 1970s, at first using GI parts almost exclusively. Later rifles use almost entirely new production parts.

International Harvester Corporation ("IHC" code). International Harvester had never built firearms before entering the program and did not deliver a rifle until late 1953, after much difficulty (including several "bailouts" by Springfield Armory, which actually produced many of the receivers). Because of marking and detail variations, the comparatively small quantities involved, and the history of the contract, the factory IHC is of little interest to shooters but fascinating to collectors (see the photo and detail sections). Serial numbers are all over 4,400,000. They are fairly common, but there are many variants/subvariants.

Pietro Beretta , Gardone, Italy ("PB" code). Though made partially on Winchester machinery, the Berettas are generally the best fitted and

PHOTO 14. The 8-round en bloc clip became one of the M1 Garand's most controversial features; almost as soon as the rifle was in production, an effort began to replace the clip with a larger, detachable magazine of greater capacity. Still, the clip was entirely contained in the rifle and carried three more rounds than most contemporary bolt action rifles.

overall best finished M1 rifles ever made, not because of any magic from the manufacturer but merely because they were made under no combat pressure, largely to revitalize an ancient and respected firearms manufactory, and because many were made competitively to export orders. Almost every part of a Beretta rifle will carry the "PB" code and, since Beretta (and Fabrique Nationale ["FN"]) rebuilt M1s for the U.S. military as early as 1947-48, it should shock no one that Beretta parts will sometimes be found on a U.S.-issue DCM rifle. The Beretta M1s are quite rare in the United States. There are no parts interchange difficulties. As is true of the Winchesters, the Berettas command a considerable price premium, which is even more profound, since price pressure (aka *demand*) comes from both collectors and shooters. The Breda-built rifles are supposedly identical, made to the same tight specifications. Although I have seen many Breda

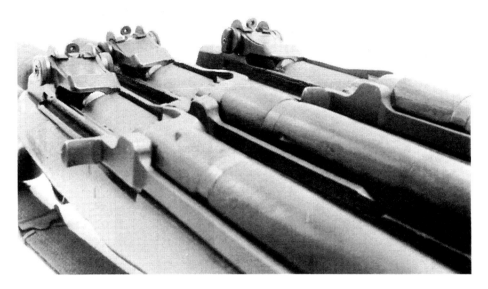

PHOTO 15. Various receiver vintages: from front, postwar, late war, and early war.

("BMB" code) parts, I have never even seen a receiver. I would not be amazed to find out there were none.

Harrington & Richardson Arms Co. ("HRA" code). All H&R receivers were built and delivered from 1953 to 1957. One fairly often finds 7.62mm barrels bearing 1956-57 dates on very high-numbered HRAs. I am inclined to believe these were ordered and delivered as such, for by the 1950s H&R had gained a good reputation with the military for delivery on time and budget and seems to have been—along with the armories—the site of much M1/M14 development. All H&R receivers were to late specification and evince excellent craftsmanship throughout. They generally come closer to a true finish match than other M1s (excepting perhaps Beretta), and the serial numbers go much higher than the oft-quoted 5,700,000 seen in collector's books. H&Rs are fairly uncommon in truly superb cosmetic condition.

THE RIFLES BY STATESIDE SOURCE

Many snobbish types in the collecting community pooh-pooh the recent post-1985 reimport rifles as little more than junk, some of this stemming from the fact that all of them must be marked with importer's data, usually on the barrel, and the fact that, unlike DCM rifles and most pre-1968 imports, these barrels are often shot out. Like most overgeneralizations, though, this easy dismissal ignores some very important facts—primarily that the recent imports represent a tremendous source of good receivers and parts. Plus, unlike with DCM rifles, one can choose a manufacturer or view the rifle before purchase. This section reviews rifles likely to be found by commercial or other source, and, while it is not complete (many thousands of M1s having entered civilian hands by other means or importers), it'll provide the reader with some handy information.

As of mid-to-late 1991, this listing covers all major M1 suppliers.

USA/DCM

The Office of the Director of Civilian Marksmanship has intermittently provided M1 Garands to match shooters and NRA members who duly qualify through their clubs under various programs since the 1950s. Current price is $310, though the program will soon end. Under some conditions, the military has released M1s to military personnel, particularly toward the end of World War II. And it has to be acknowledged that some M1s left military ownership via extremely unauthorized means and can no longer be identified.

While all these rifles, if not modified, are "original issue," they have customarily seen some replacement of parts and/or updating/rebuilding, and may be in any parameter of condition. Significantly, they will not bear any physical identification as to source. In the last several months I've seen several anomalies in DCM M1s, all shipped since 1988: a complete, correct, totally unmodified lend-lease M1 ca. 1942 in mint condition with uncut operating rod; a Navy 7.62x51 Match rifle, pristine and properly bedded, with H&R receiver and birch stock; a grungy, disgusting Springfield with partially mashed gas cylinder, stock pounded badly, but no pitting and a virtually new ca. 1944 barrel (the barrel could be sold for more than the rifle's price to a collector who needed it, by the way); two very nice World War II vintage Springfield Armory M1s, one with all the Korean War vintage updates but, oddly, a WRA bolt, the other substantially unmodified; and a collector-correct IHC rifle, very nice, mint barrel, but totally incapable of holding 4 MOA on paper, even with match ammunition.

Before a DCM rifle is sent, it is certified in "service condition." This certification is not the detailed check conducted by armorers when the gun was still in active service, but it at least assures the recipient that stocks will not be cracked in key areas, that parts work, and that the barrel is not excessively worn or eroded.

Pre-1968 Imports

M1s were sold or sent to many countries following World War II, partially due to Cold War pressures, but also because the Fascist forces stole all the local firearms and left their conquests unarmed. Since the Axis Powers' firearms—mostly left where they were dropped in defeat—were generic to parts and ammunition of out-of-business powers, the United States and England—and, in some of the world, the Soviet Union—rearmed the world. By the sixties, M1 was viewed as too heavy, too powerful, and, since it was out of production, a military lame duck. M1s began to arrive from Belgium, Germany, Italy, and elsewhere not long before the Gun Control Act of 1968 (GCA '68) cut off all surplus imports. As a group, these may be the best of all M1s, though they are also uncommon. Not marked as to origin, save where the recipient country attached some legend (usually in the buttstock), these rifles are very unlikely to have seen much use or heavy reconditioning/refinishing. Some rare rifles entered, too, including one IHC I have seen with British proofs. This was not a lend-lease rifle (IHC didn't produce any rifles until 1953) but was either used in British duty with some U.S.-NATO attached unit or was in the UK on some nonmilitary function, for British proof laws require "resident" firearms be proofed and marked before even leaving customs. These guns carried very high prices for the time.

REMILs

In the 1950s, when M1 parts were cheap and plentiful, there were essentially no receivers on the open market. Uncle Sam had determined that the best way to get rid of the leftovers from World War II and Korea was to torch them or saw them in half. However, some welders, machinists, weapons buffs, and dealers thought it might be a good idea to buy some of these pieces as scrap and see if the parts glut could be manipulated to produce some complete weapons. Back then this was all legal and more or less aboveboard. It began with machine guns, which even then had to be registered when completed. Fixture alignment was critical; sometimes little pieces had to fabricated, and about 50 percent of the assembled-reassembled receivers were junked (many of these were salvaged by less reputable dealers and resold). Naturally, the fronts and rears of the receivers didn't necessarily match by maker or style, so often late and early fronts and rears were butted together, even from different manufacturers. Much grinding and polishing was necessary to get these in a functionable condition, and a "bump"—either in the ridge line of the clip ejector recess area or the operating rod track on the receiver's right side—is the surest clue to a REMIL. Often, barrels had to be tack-welded in place because many of the receivers were already worn out. These are today the least valuable M1 receivers, though this does not mean they cannot shoot accurately and well. Some of the less reputable manufacturers even sleeved and arc welded two-groove Springfield barrels just ahead of the M1 barrel stub—another dead giveaway, for no M1 barrel was made with two grooves. On the plus side, I've seen REMIL M1s with proper setup shoot excellent match scores. But these were extensively checked and modified guns. Any reweld is suspect, not

PHOTO 16. Garands as received from the importer, all with "type 3" rear sights, representing (from left) mid-World War II, pre-war ca. 1940, and late World War II receivers. Note the "seam" on the rightmost receiver, this line being apparently the effect of a worn mill blade stopping at the receiver's top ridge contour with each stroke, repeatedly. This line does not adversely impact the receiver's strength or value, and, in fact, the receivers like this that were examined were about .008 inch thicker in the rear "horseshoe" area than others. Note also the large, flat area of the postwar replacement stock, apparently designed to accept the revised selective fire, Remington-developed receiver, which never saw production. Note also small contour details among the various receivers.

because of class outfits like P&S, which checked all of its REMILs for straightness, hardness, and measurement specifications, but because of the bootleggers who pervaded the market with truly slipshod work.

Police Reimports

Once GCA '68 was in effect, no military-owned firearm could be imported into the United States. However, there was an exemption for police officers and police-use items, and thus considerable numbers of H&R and IHC M1s (as well as the more common Springfields) got into the United States, primarily from Latin America, where they seem to have seen almost no use or modification. Some of these rifles carry the marks of the importers who brought them in; most do not. Most seem to have entered with new wood, primarily "SA" marked and cartouched. I have seen only a few, but all were essentially perfect mechanically and cosmetically, either rebuilt to new condition stateside or mint from shipment south to return north.

The Post '85 Era

In 1985, significant modifications to the Gun Control Act of 1968 allowed reimportation/importation to the U.S. market of all firearms then on the official Curios and Relics list, among which were M1s. Since the beginning of the Military Aid Program (MAP) in the late 1940s, however, shipment to the United States of any significant materials acquired from U.S. military sources (substantially with taxpayer dollars) has been prohibited. After many customs, BATF, and other hassles and legal battles, however, this provision—intended to keep some of the more corrupt of our "allies" from enhancing their personal fortunes at the expense of the American taxpayer—was relaxed for what American shooters knew to be obsolescent military hardware, of use only to shooters and collectors.

This section is intended to be helpful in identifying Garands brought in since 1985. All such firearms are stamped with the importer's name or letter code, home city, and caliber. A summary follows, and, again, it is undoubtedly not complete, for many other small lots have entered.

Century Arms ("CAI" code). These rifles came from Italy, northern Africa, and China. Conditions run the gamut, but they were not freshly refinished just before or after entry, the lots were not very big, and most barrels are sound.

Blue Sky Productions ("Blue Sky" code). These rifles came from South Korea. Most barrels were not good; some even showed evidence of having been polished with high-speed rigs before refinish. Virtually all were refinished freshly before resale. Some markings are better than others. This lot includes many rare and/or unusual rifles, but most saw major rebuilds and so, for the collector, are mostly parts sources. To the shooter, however, these rebuilds are advantageous, for the later operating rods and other parts found on most of these rifles are superior performers and considerably less likely to be worn out. Many stocks are repaired with pins (a fix that was mechanically successful but cosmetically unappealing). Many are cracked and unrepaired. Many "NM" operating rods are seen on service rifles.

Federal Ordnance Incorporated ("Fed Ord" code). These rifles came from the Phillipines. Many were pitted in noncritical areas due to the humid climate, and virtually all were oxide-refinished before stateside resale. The importer applied markings on the front receiver strut rather than on the barrel. The wood was generally sanded heavily before resale, removing virtually all markings. Most barrels are better than those of Blue Sky rifles, and more than half I have seen were new or virtually new. These tend to be good shooters "as is," but ugly.

Sherwood/Samco (several codes). These rifles were brought in from Israel by Sherwood and Samco virtually as soon as the law changed. Having spent parts of their careers in countries as diverse as West Germany and Yugoslavia (the Israelis apparently purchased some from the United States and some from Europe), these rifles have many odd parts but are of very high quality. Do not be surprised to find German, Yugoslav, or FN-Belgian barrels on these. There are many M1Ds, some M1Cs in this batch, most of them probably field-modified to that specification but technically correct. Some M1C variants with 1-inch rings (probably USMC units by Griffin & Howe [G&H]) were in this lot, but without the glass. This lot was genuinely superb, and most of the rifles remain in splendid condition.

Arlington Ordnance ("Arl Ord" or similar code). Many Garands and M1 Carbines bear this mark. Relatively late entries into the surplus market, the guns primarily come from Korea. These guns were not subjected to new refinishes before import unless it was really necessary, meaning there is a greater chance of finding an original finish rifle among these than among some others. More than 50 of these rifles were purchased in preparation for this book and examined in great detail. They were generally in better-than-average condition and import marked with some care and subtlety. Among them were several original, unmodified postwar rifles and a large number of almost original World War II rifles that were easily restored, including the Winchesters, H&Rs, and late Springfields heavily illustrated herein. Jack Williams, marketing director for Arlington Ordnance, advises me that it is Arlington's intention to quality control the rifles as far as fit and safety and not to interfere with old refinishes or original finish (whereas most of the Blue Sky guns were refinished pro forma). My favorite match gun is an Arlington Ord M1 ca. 1954, fitted with appropriate match parts. These are the best large lots of Garands available at the time of this writing.

Springfield Sporters ("SPR SP" code). Most of these rifles came from Colombia. They were received by the Colombians from the United States and Europe, and they include some Berettas. There are many "gray"—unmarked, probably U.S.-MAP supplied—barrels on these rifles. All stateside-ordered rebuilds and specifications seem to have been adhered to, and there is no general pattern of receiver refinishing. These rifles all seem to have excellent barrels and are one of the best choices for the owner who wishes to shoot his rifle "as-is" and immediately. Should the shooter/collector wish to upgrade, restore, or match prepare a less-than-perfect M1 Garand, data provided in the last part of this text will give considerable information that will be of use. Suffice it to say, an M1 for $250 is almost always not a bargain, whereas one for $500-600 may actually be cheap. It depends on what the rifle actually is, and what the intended use happens to be. Almost no M1 from any of these subcategories is really a "piece of junk," but it may very well have some pieces of junk hanging on it.

THE OLD RIFLE REJUVENATED:
THE SAFE, ACCURATE, SMART, COMPLETE M1

While it's true that most any M1 receiver can be transformed into a reliable, straight-shooting rifle eventually, the process is not necessarily easy or cheap. Little known to collectors, who are sometimes even shooting rifles with original World War II bolts and unmodified operating rods, the process of shooting the M1 is also not necessarily safe. In fact, Technical Operational Orders issued to armorers from 1947 to 1949 ordered the replacement of all original operating rods and/or the addition of a hemispherical cutout at the first rearward 90-degree joint, since some deaths and injuries had been caused by the operating rods' breakage at that point. In the mid-1950s similar information demanding local inspection of IHC- and WRA-marked bolts for signs of bending, and of IHC operating rods for excessive hardness, was also dispensed. These are situations where the meaning behind specifications was locally misinterpreted or mishandled by the manufacturer. The IHC operating rods are not all defective, but the recent appearance on the civilian market of large numbers of new IHC rods causes one to wonder if these might be the ones in question. *Most* of the Winchester bolts I have seen and/or inspected showed the "too soft lug, too hard boltface" problem. Obviously, though the bending was already well along on the lugs, not all of these were destroyed or discarded as they were supposed to be. This is fortunate for collectors, unfortunate for shooters.

All the usual admonitions about headspace and ammunition applied to other arms, particularly semiautos, apply especially to the M1. But other specifications, such as gas cylinder integrity, size of gas vent (different in 7.62 and .30/06 rifles), lubrication (heavy grease, heavy grease only, and enough of it), condition of follower spring (most people call it the "recoil spring," which is what it really is), and general cleanliness of the bore and gas system must also be checked and adhered to.

Nowhere in any modern manual is oil mentioned as a lubricant, and that's 100-percent correct. Using oil on an M1 receiver is what truly bends operating rods and breaks parts. Use grease.

The most expensive parts on the M1 Garand are the operating rod, barrel, gas cylinder, and stock. The most likely to fail is the follower/operating rod spring (recoil spring). A troubleshooting chart analyzing M1 glitches is included at the end of this book. It can be quickly summarized, though, by noting that an operating rod catch, bullet guide, follower/recoil spring, firing pin, and extractor are the most necessary spare parts. Clumsy folks who insist upon stripping the bolt in a hurry should order the ejector in multiples. Unrestrained, this heavily sprung part can be propelled with great velocity and—if not imbedded in the shooter's person—easily lost. For civilian shooters—and particularly for those who shoot the shorter, lighter 7.62x51 round—the ejector spring can be safely trimmed by two coils. Stock Garands fling brass 20 or more feet, which was handy for the military but likely means nothing to you. Polishing the extractor surface means your brass is less likely to be damaged, and it will be located more uniformly as well. Where for parts? Check Part IV of this text. The remainder of this section breaks important parts down into information convenient for the shooter and likely useful for the collector as well.

Barrels

Garand barrels are expensive, and the wise shooter should appreciate that the cheapest of today's barrels will outperform even mint original GI issue from more than 40 years ago. The best of the civilian aftermarket heavy barrels can produce a whole new category of accuracy—and last longer to boot. Service bolt guns can't compete with the prepared Garand for accuracy, and, despite sniveling to the contrary, the Springfield '03 match rifles with match ammo couldn't equal the performance of selected but unaltered M1s with postwar service ammo. A new, high-quality custom barrel can put the semiautomatic Garand into a speed-with-accuracy combination not many other long guns can even approach. However, those who both collect and compete would be wise to pursue these activities with separate rifles. A Douglas or Krieger heavy profile match barrel on a properly prepared M1 may cost less than a ca. 1955 Springfield "NM" in pristine condition but will shoot far better and last longer to boot. That's why Marine Corps and Navy match teams began ordering special equipment outside ordinary mass procurement channels as early as 1951.

There is another important footnote about the Garand: provided you can afford the ammo, M1 tends to be shot more and in less time than most rifles. At 2,600+ feet per second (fps), copper fouling very quickly becomes a problem. I've bought "shot out" M1s to which accuracy was restored instantly by careful treatment with copper solvents and/or Outers' reverse electroplate process. Williams sells a particularly handy copper solvent in a handy, unbreakable bottle that goes with me where my M1s go. I also use Kleenbore Copper Cutter and Hoppe's #9 in the Benchrest Copper Solvent version.

Now the barrels, by brand and category.

GI

Government issue and military aid program M1 barrels were produced by about everyone who could bore and contour the stock and cut the rifling. Winchester replacement barrels (mostly ca. 1953-64), use "electric writing" logo style and are sometimes mistaken for issue barrels. They sell for absurdly high prices. Marlin, Savage, Remington, and many others produced replacement barrels, as did all the major contractors. Virtually all were four-groove, though I have seen five- and six-groove replacement units with military markings and one Marlin with many-groove "button" rifling. There were *no* two-groove M1 barrels, though some shady operators welded and recontoured combinations of shot-out M1 rifles and two-groove Springfield barrels and sold them as originals. Collectors will pay high prices for original barrels, but to the shooter they just aren't worth much. A Winchester barrel, original or replacement, which can cost up to $500, will not perform as well as the $120-150 civilian barrel. GI match barrels are not much better than standard units unless they are of very late vintage.

Heavy Match

Unquestionably, the best barrel for the M1 is the Wisconsin-built Krieger. Douglas is a close second. The Krieger is "very heavy," which demands reducing the rear handguard to a mere shell. The Douglas is only slightly smaller, and the handguard must be similarly sanded or routed. Both are available as stainless units, and both can be had in 7.62x51 (.308). Both should be ordered short chambered and then finish chambered to the shooter's bolt and receiver by a smith or armorer. Olympic/Safari Arms markets a barrel similar to the Douglas, which I have not had an opportunity to test. Douglas offers six grooves as an option. Citadel offers a similar barrel in four or six grooves. These are the most durable and accurate M1 barrels, though also the hardest to fit and the most expensive.

Standard Configuration

Springfield Armory, Incorporated offers new barrels of six-groove pattern in both calibers to a slightly enhanced GI specification and also has a "match" specification version. The match units cost $40 more. Both are excellent. The option of four grooves is listed but apparently is not actually available. Citadel and others offer service and match barrels of standard configuration for very reasonable prices, but there are some borderline crooks out there selling rejects and remarked barrels at high prices.

Wood is an easily solved problem. I use Fajen stocks on my fancy guns, and lately prices on the stocks alone as well as on complete sets have been falling. At the time of this writing, there is a great deal of good, issue walnut on the market at very low prices. There are also plastic stocks available (see the data in the marketplace section of Part IV). It is wise to have spare handguards.

The late-issue match sight set used on the Garand was introduced in 1962. Many surplus dealers stock them. The hooded aperture can be used with the service base and knobs but will not give fine adjustments. (See the match section in Part II for details.)

M1D barrels with blocks are now available new and used, and M1C drilling jigs are on the market. The wisest way to scope an M1 is probably with B-Square's unit, which doesn't require modifying the rifle.

BMF-Activator's Straightpull York Conversion kit changes the old semiauto into a straightpull bolt gun and saves several pounds of weight along the way. One advantage to the unit is that those parts that are hardest to clean are not on the rifle in its hunting, straightpull condition.

Smith/Western Ordnance in Tempe, Arizona, markets a compensator/muzzle brake for the Garand, furnished in Parkerized external finish, very convenient for extended practice fire, with no deleterious effect on accuracy. It seems to increase my shoulder endurance by about 10 to 20 percent. This unit replaces the gas cylinder lock and somewhat modernizes the old service rifle's appearance.

Smiths around the country market services to convert M1 into a sort of BM.59 clone, just as Beretta did 30 years or so ago. This is handy, but the 20-round magazine capacity may cause users to run afoul of the gun confiscation lobby when it has its next couple of twitches.

.308/7.62 NATO conversions, however, are easy, handy, economical, and smart. Only a barrel change is required. The chamber bushings, sooner or later, will cause problems. The magazine spacers are not necessary, but if one operates rifles in both calibers, they will prevent the nightmare jams which occur when a .30/06 round meets a .308 chamber. The newer, shorter cartridge is more efficient, less powder-intensive, generates less gross heat, and, despite a higher chamber pressure, generates less down the spout—which is why about 1/64-inch enlargement of the gas port is required. Most important of all (as discussed elsewhere in this book), high-quality practice ammo is everywhere and cheap.

Practical Parts for the Practical Man

The most common malfunction of the M1 Garand is the premature dumping of the clip, accompanied by one or more live cartridges. (See the troubleshooting guide and Photo 21 in Part II.) Actually, the most common breakage is the snapping of the recoil spring, but, surprisingly, this often does not eventuate any malfunction at all. With the early ejection difficulty, the clip late/clip ejector mechanism is never the problem. The correct fix prescribed in all manuals is the replacement of the bullet guide and the operating rod catch. Both should be replaced simultaneously. These are not expensive parts. Stamped bullet guides, which tend to work better, sell for as little as $2, and the operating rod catch is seldom more than $10. Procedures for replacement are outlined in the manual included in this book. The time involved should be less than three minutes.

Contrary to conventional wisdom, match M1s are less fussy mechanically than even the robust Garand service rifle, if clean and properly lubricated with grease and otherwise correctly prepared.

"Special" parts and preparations on National Match or "Civvy" accuracy rifles are generally as follows (as detailed in the National Match section of this book): 1) all wood relieved so as not to impinge directly on barrel, receiver, operating rod, or gas cylinder; 2) gas cylinder upper "hoop" bored out and shortened, so as not to contact handguard ferrule or barrel; 3) middle band and often handguard ferrule secure to front ("upper") handguard, after boring or sanding out same to free float front of barrel; 4) trigger pull cleaned up, deburred, and if/when necessary, lightened to normal minimum of 4.5 pounds very clean pull; 5) tin operating rod guide/sleeve thrown away, though lately, I have seen some merely highly polished and drilled for heat relief on nicely working rifles; 6) stacking swivel's rear tab undercut, beveled, or otherwise reduced to eliminate any and all interference with the front handguard and/or handguard ferrule; 7) fitting of M1/M14 NM2A sight set, complete with knobs and bases, normally both front and rear; 8) often, exact and precise mating and lapping of bolt/barrel/chamber interface; 9) glass or epoxy bedding of the rifle's action and trigger group area, and, often, relief of the front well of the buttstock, or replacement of same with a polymer surface to minimize swelling and damage.

Certain other fits are often done to make M1 more reliable. Often, key moving parts are black-chromed or polymerized or hard-chromed—in particular the operating rod, bolt, and hammer. The military frequently marked bolts and trigger groups with the last three or four digits of the receiver serial number rather crudely with a scratch awl. Barrels were frequently, but not always, marked "NM," or sometimes "HG" (High Grade) on the left front, about 2 inches back from the front, upper "hoop" of the gas cylinder.

Most of these same detailed procedures were also followed with the later M14, many parts of which will interchange with the earlier rifle. The NM2A sights, in fact, were primarily intended for the M14.

Many of these operations can be done by anyone with minimal hand tool skills.

M1 FODDER AND FEED: AMMO FOR THE WARHORSE

The M1 Garand is a rifle with two personalities: the military rifle (rough 'n' tumble, the collector's darling) and the shooting thorough-bred (still tough, but precise and accurate). It is therefore appropriate for the shooter who owns more than one gun or who enjoys both endeavors to—as I do—clearly define two diets for his classic. There's plain old powder-burning, high-powered plinking, and then there's truly precise shooting.

For fairly casual shooting, there's no reason to be afraid of corrosive ammunition, provided one is willing to wash away the salts created by the primers. The proper and fast way is with a window-cleaner-like solution of detergent, water, ammonia, and alcohol followed by a normal cleaning with conventional solvents and brushes. The ammoniated solution is best applied while the bore is still hot to warm. Another vital step in prolonging barrel life and preserving accuracy is an aggressive attack on copper fouling. Specialized copper solvents and Outers' reverse electroplate kit are very helpful.

M1 runs dirty. Leaving it that way is never smart.

How you get it that way—having fun with the rifle—involves shooting what you aim at. Despite a great deal of Internet hooey to the contrary, the very best loads for the Garand are those calculated specifically for the rifle—and that means handloads, executed by a careful shooter who knows and follows the rules. But there are many alternatives. The first choice to make is, of course, which kind of cartridge to purchase or load.

There just isn't much low-cost, quality .30/06 on the market, and supplies must inherently decline as this now obsolete military loading dwindles on the surplus market. In recent years shooters have snapped up lots of Dominican ammo (actually, mostly made by Remington and almost entirely Boxer-primed), FN from Belgium, and ancient M1 and M2 ball and ca. 1942 armor piercing. French Gevelot is corrosive, and most of it is quite good, but like all French ammunition, powder stability can be a problem. Recent "remanufactured" military ball and armor piercing ammo from Gibbs/Navy Arms is fully reloadable and better than old M2 ball but will probably sell out soon. The Austrian ball ammunition on the market is fine but expensive. The Dutch ball is way too expensive and costs more than brand new commercial ammo.

Among commercial items, the PrviPartizan I acquire from Century has performed well and is still quite reasonably priced. Federal's American Eagle is sensibly priced—cheaper than most surplus. Of course, Federal's Gold Match—at about a dollar a shot—is the standard by which all others are measured but is surely not plinking ammo for most of us. Occasionally some original GI .30/06 match becomes available, but it will not equal the Federal loading.

7.62x51 NATO (the slightly different commercial equivalent is .308 Winchester) ammunition poses far less mystery. Cheap, high-quality practice ammo is virtually ubiquitous, and virtually every maker in the world produces supplies of premium quality ammunition at competitive prices. The Argentine, Belgian, Israeli, Spanish, and Venezuelan surplus ammo from Century Arms is all suitable. The corrosive rounds from the Eastern Bloc are also fine but require the special cleaning procedures outlined earlier.

Federal's Gold Match is available in this loading, too. But Winchester and Remington also produce high-quality precision loads using 168-grain match bullets in the .308 caliber. All are superb.

When it's time for ultra-serious shooting, handloads are the prescription. Of late, my primary powders in both calibers are IMR 4064, Hodgdon's VARGET, Hodgdon BLC-2, and Accurate Arms 2520. Generally, 168-grain to 190-grain match profile boattail hollowpoints are the bullets of choice, with IMI's bulk package 150-grain boattail hard-nose providing an economical alternative. The best accuracy is always available with 165-grain and heavier projectiles.

I have lately standardized on Federal's Gold Match 210GM primer for ball powders and CCI's Benchrest Large Rifle for all other powders.

Semiautomatic rifles are somewhat more sensitive to pressure permutations than bolt actions: too little, and the gun will not run; too much and (if something doesn't get broken), at the very least, the brass may not land in the same county. Avoid 4350 and anything slower in full-power loads for the Garand, the M14, or any similar gas-operated rifles (though with reduced loads, at about a .30/30 power level, they work fine). This comes from a coincidence of their development of highest heat precisely where the gas ports live.

Sierra's manuals include accuracy data, though the loads chosen may not be appropriate for the Garand.

Much of the voodoo about M1 match loads consists of, if not bunk, then, at the very least, strange exaggerations. The GI match information suggests strongly that if 168-175 grain match bullets are held in the velocity range of 2,580-2,630 fps, accuracy will be close to optimal. That's more or less regardless of the powder or brass used, provided charges are precisely uniform and case volume and condition are carefully checked for consistency. Most any brass will suffice, but any and all controls to test for uniform weight and volume will pay off downrange.

Many combinations can work well, but the components must be as uniform as possible. "Batching" cases by weight and volume is important. Though it's true that I get fine results with setups claimed "inappropriate" for a caliber (especially in the Garand), my long-range findings are that consistency from one round to the next few means a great deal in consistent point or impact and, therefore, scores and group size.

One often-heard bit of poppycock—tested empirically and found to be false—concerns the use of match ammunition in service rifles. The slightly heavier bullets have no negative impact at all. Pressures are, if anything, a bit lower. Lousy lubrication—that is, no lubrication, wrong lubricants, or insufficient lubrication—causes the bent operating rod syndrome sometimes associated with heavier bullets. It is, however, true that loading heavier bullets, even at comparatively low pressures and velocities, can beat up an M1—especially the operating rod. Surprisingly, this effect is often more profound with lower-pressure loads, and, again, the reason is simply understood through a little discussion of the physics involved. A bullet moving at, say, 1,200 fps (as a 230-grain slug might be in a Garand) exposes the entire gas system to pressure for more than twice as much time as a bullet at 2,600 fps+. There is, therefore, a tendency for the operating rod to be under rearward force long after it's fully back. Even this seems to be partially nullified by the use of heavy grease on the top rod rail of the receiver.

In 1986 I concocted an experiment to test the "bendability" of the M1 operating rod. From a retailer in Los Angeles, I acquired some 700 rounds of Browning 220-grain roundnose .30/06 loads. These I ran through an ancient, pitted M1 with a straight but pitted operating rod. After 691 rounds I had no bending, no malfunction, and no signs of serious peening. I was using an automotive MDS/graphite bearing grease rather heavily. Somewhat annoyed at being unable to induce a problem I had been told would become obvious in 20 rounds, I used turpentine to remove all the grease. Seven rounds later, the oiled rifle—remember, I told you about wrong lubricants—couldn't even be properly disassembled without heavy force, for the operating rod was on the brink of breakage, the spring had broken, and the right front bolt lug was heavily peened. Point proven, I gave the two remaining loaded rounds to a man firing a Remington 700 lightweight—he may still be angry with me—and satisfied myself that another little bit of scuttlebutt had been disproved.

A good M1 match barrel—and the military followed this pattern in M1 and M14 preparations—should get continuously more accurate for about 3,500 rounds. The tube should remain at a very high level for about 10,000 rounds. This can be extended greatly by careful cleaning and can be greatly compressed by failing to clean properly or by radical, repeated rapid firing. Without cleaning, a tight M1 match barrel will evince seriously compromised accuracy after only a few hundred rounds. Copper fouling impacts all high-velocity barrels and must be fought constantly. The higher the velocity, the more rapid the fire; the higher the heat, the worse the problem becomes.

With regular cleaning, gas ports do not corrode, though they tend to erode from heat about the time the barrel finally dies.

Slower-burning powders leave more residue in the gas system. Ball powders leave less residue than extruded powders of similar speed.

For handloaders who like to practice regularly, a good procedure is to work up a 150- or 168-grain load barely sufficient to operate the rifle. This will reduce fatigue on the shooter and rifle (the lower velocities contribute less copper fouling), and the good habits that come only from practice can thus be enjoyed more cheaply and with less work afterward. Each Garand will react differently, but with proper, heavy grease lubricants (*never* use oil, especially not on the receiver grooves and bolt corners) and a good polish on the upper surface of the operating rod, it is often amazing how little powder/pressure is required to operate this big, old, ugly rifle.

Even the old adage about heavy bullets tending to break or compromise the rifle is not necessarily correct if sensible caution is exercised. More details follow in subsequent sections of this book.

STRAIGHT AND TRUE DOWNRANGE: M1 GARAND AND ACCURACY

The military match manual for the specialized preparation of the M1 Garand is included later in this book, so it would be redundant to fully explore those processes here. Indeed, to diehard collectors, attempting such a recreation is blasphemous. A good, handy guide to quick accurizing of the Garand is included in the NRA's *The M1 Rifle*. However, even the "if it ain't issue, it ain't M1" hardnose should at least read the information in this section, for it explains some characteristics of the rifle that were once fairly mysterious and outlines the philosophy employed in setting up the accuracy rifle.

When the M1 first appeared in match competition in 1939 and 1940, any observer could quite reasonably and surely surmise that the M1's $92+ procurement price was plain, simple wasted money. The Roosevelt administration had persevered with the new spreading of firepower downward in the face of heavy opposition from inside the military, and the old "boondoggle" word was appearing again. A lot of tweaking was necessary to make the M1 into the rifle World War II vets remember so fondly. Later, more research would eliminate the strange and erratic patterns of inaccuracy some rifles evinced. The rhythmic stoppage problem was gone by late 1941. But often, rifles would evince strange flyers, putting (typically) one bullet in eight somewhere divorced from intended point of impact. The more loosely the wood was fitted, the less this seemed to happen. By the 1960s it was discovered that oddments of stress and torque on barrel and receiver, especially when the rifle got hot, were responsible. Since, match-prepared rifles have used an extensive list of relief modifications to stand off wood and metal while bedding holds the receiver firm.

Glass or epoxy bedding—I prefer the new epoxies—has been the standard first step to match prepare M1 for at least 35 years. Derrick Martin, a first-class riflesmith and Perry competitor, puts it simply: "A lot of simplistic, expensive fixes go on the wrong end of the rifle. A new barrel will almost always improve an M1, but glass bedding costs less and can often result in even more improvement."

Of course, also back there at the shooter's end of the rifle are the trigger, chamber/bolt and therefore headspace, and the operating rod rails, which can, if severely worn, mess up everything the rifle does, including shooting straight.

To me, a match-prepared M1 done by a first-class civilian smith is a relative bargain, and the logical place to begin the improvements is right there where you stick your face. I stress "civilian-prepared" because my experience with "authentic" M1 match rifles is that they belong with collectors. I've owned many, and most needed lots of fixing because they'd been improperly prepared or shot to death. Even a pristine ca. 1965 SA-updated gun wouldn't shoot close to *any* of my civilian prepared rifles until I set aside its issue National Match barrel and replaced it with a Douglas. Bear in mind that it met every shooting and mechanical specification and measurement, but while it was much more accurate than a run-of-the-mine M1, just replacing the barrel cut it from a "sometime" MOA shooter that could not hold a group when it got hot to a consistent sub-MOA gun that took 40 or more rounds to show any heat reaction at all. Had it been a 7.62, I might still own it. But it was .30/06, and it left my ownership with two barrels.

Therein lies a small lesson. An M1 can be both a war curio and a target gun, if one is wise enough to save the alternate parts. First quality Navy and Marine match rifles in 7.62 are now bringing as much as $1,000, but most shooters want to test-fire such guns. Service guns in mint condition command $400 to $600. Neither is common. The $200+ wall hanger may properly belong permanently in a rack, but it can be made to look and shoot better than most civilians can even understand, and some of this is a small matter of elbow grease.

This most famous and successful of all U.S. military rifles has much brilliant history behind it, but its best days may well prove to be in the 21st century.

II
THE PRACTICAL M1 GARAND

After you unpack your M1, loading it up and shooting it are not your next steps. Learning how not to break it must be your next logical move.

That said, in the following sections you will find some rules of thumb, a heavily documented and researched military trouble shooting/analysis chart with notes (reprinted from an army manual), and the Beretta version of the military manual written late in the rifle's life that is the best "quickie" manual I've seen. Some small parts of it are a little dated, but it's presented here intact. The photos will help you deal with terminology and grasp the procedures involved in maintaining the rifle properly.

Remember: there would be far less appliances in the trash, fewer cars in the junkyard, and poorer mechanics and plumbers if consumers paid some attention to the instructions packed with almost everything they buy. The M1 is no more complex to maintain than any other firearm, but since it runs fast and strong, and since everything that can happen is well documented, the value of the rifle dictates preventive maintenance. Commercial semiautos are far more fragile, nowhere near as easily serviced, and not as much fun to shoot—nor do they feature as much history. Use the information. It will save you money and maybe even secure your health.

QUICK RULES OF THUMB (AND OTHER BODY PARTS) IN THE CARE AND MAINTENANCE OF JOHN GARAND'S BIG, HEAVY RIFLE

1. Never—under any circumstances—use oil to lubricate any major part of the M1 Garand. Use grease—heavy grease—in the four bolt points, op rod channel/receiver raceway, and op rod detent. I use a

high-temperature, high-pressure wheel bearing grease, for which I pay $1.99 to $3.50 per tub at an auto parts store. You can buy the same thing in itty-bitty, teensy-weensy canisters labeled for firearms use at $3.50 per quarter-ounce, if you wish. Using no lubricants (or improper ones) will seriously attack your rifle's systems. Oil will slop onto the stock and you and just generally make a mess, without doing anything to help the rifle. Incorrect lubricants contribute to the premature death of operating rods, receivers, and, sometimes, shooters.

2. If one shoots corrosive ammo, bores must be swabbed or flushed with water/detergent solutions, preferably with ammonia added, followed by a solvent cleaning shortly thereafter. As with any high-velocity rifle whose owner wishes it to last any serious length of time, a copper fouling procedure must also follow extensive shooting *every single time the rifle is fired*. Although these techniques were controversial 50 years ago, benchrest shooters have demonstrated absolutely and empirically their value in prolonging barrel life and sustaining accuracy.

3. Never, under any circumstances, sand a military Garand stock that retains any original markings, and, most especially, use no abrasives in areas where the markings and stampings actually reside. This is a serious depreciation of the stock's value. Especially if one sands in the area where the receiver contacts wood, inaccuracy and cracking will become a problem, and very quickly.

4. There is seldom need to remove the gas cylinder, even for cleaning. However, if it is removed and reinstalled there is no need for it to contact the front handguard and/or ferrule, and, in fact, doing so can and will have a deleterious impact on accuracy. Minor peens on the channels that align and secure the cylinder can be used to resecure a loose gas cylinder, whose slop will definitely cause larger-than-necessary groups, since the front sight reposes up topside. Suggested standoff from handguard ferrule: .040 inch

5. Actually shooting original, unrelieved World War II operating rods is unwise, dangerous, and financially silly. They can work fine—right up until the time they break and kill you. This may be one round away, it may be 5,000 rounds away, but the laws of stress and physics do not change. The least a separation will cost you is your boyish good looks and maybe a nose or an eye. Lefties usually die. Plus, these old-timers are worth money. Use the parts photos in this section to identify yours. Spare operating rods are not as expensive as major surgery.

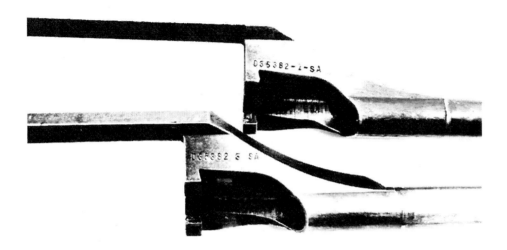

PHOTO 17. Use of uncut operating rods for the M1 Garand (these are two very early units) is dangerous and unnecessary. However, do not alter valuable originals. Simply purchase a relieved wartime specimen or a later postwar unit in nice condition. Note the uninterrupted square corner about 1/2 inch above the part number on these old units and the crude welding, especially on the -1 unit (top).

PHOTO 18. This "cut" (modified with hemispherical cut to relieve stress) Winchester wartime operating rod is far safer than unmodified originals, though of far less collector value.

6. The "correct" finish for the wood parts of the M1 Garand and most other military rifles is pure tung or linseed oil, sometimes mixed with glossy spar varnish. These are inherently shiny finishes that flatten down with age and exposure to heat and light. The matte finish many veterans remember or think they remember is nothing more than the ravages of time, ignorance, and neglect. Other fin-

ishes, such as lacquers, may be applied, but total lack of finish—which is what these old salts actually recall—is unwise, will cause accuracy and staining problems, and will ultimately cause the stock to crack.

7. With the correct gas system, .243, .308, .25/06, .270, and other caliber Garands can and do work absolutely beautifully. However, properly mashed up and dinged by a well-meaning fool or one of the "I always wanted to fix a real rifle" crowd, even the .30/06 is iffy. M1 has suffered far more from derelict owners, clumsy smiths, and bad advice from various publishers who should know better than it ever has from any design deficiency or set of inherent glitches. The rifle is far sturdier than the M14 or any cast clone thereof, and it is surely the strongest semiautomatic high-powered rifle ever built. But some people can and do break anything, and they continually apply their ignorance, lack of skill, and bigger and better hammers to an ever more vast and continuing variety of inappropriate objects and devices. Idiots are what primarily and profoundly impact machinery, from your family car to your M1 Garand. If need be, pay them to stay the hell away from your rifle and everything else you own. You can, ultimately, destroy your property yourself . . . why pay a premium to someone else to do it for you?

8. Post World War II rifles (serial numbers about 4,200,000 and higher, or Berettas) are considerably stronger than earlier guns; are far less likely to have been mashed up, dropped, or fired in anger than earlier guns; and have probably missed the clumsy attentions of at least one or two generations of that primary destroyer of military hardware, the clumsy recruit.

9. The original metal finish on almost everything M1 is some sort of phosphate. However, parkerizing—the GI name for the finish—took many forms and many different depths and colors according to the materials to which it was applied and the needs of the particular part. Even underlying polish level changed the color and reflectivity of the finish. The phosphate was post-application treated in many different ways. Barrels, for example, were usually a different shade from receivers and sights. Most M1s left the factories far darker than the medium gray so common now. Most Garands were delivered with a rather dark base finish, somewhere between a very dark gray to charcoal and black. Winchester receivers and most other parts were black. Few rifles bore an absolutely uniform finish, and a uniform medium gray is a virtually certain sign that a rifle has been refinished—probably fairly recently.

PHOTO 19. The military M1 TEG (throat erosion gauge) inserted in old ca. 1948 rebuild of any early World War II rifle, evincing an excellent 2.5 reading.

PHOTO 20. The M1 Garand TEG is the only reliable way to judge the condition of a military Garand barrel, and its information is far more vital than the degree of crud in the bore or the bore's polish condition. The numbers here index bore condition. Anything over five is heavily worn. However, because civilian barrels use gentler leades (one of several reasons they last so much longer and shoot better), even high-quality units may read 5 even when brand new.

10. Want to lose a thumb? The Garand can relieve you of an excess digit and inflict more pain in a heartbeat than you ever want to know about. Good pointers: a) your bolt is not fully back until it's fully back; b) pressure on the follower required to trip/release the bolt becomes less as the rifle wears, virtually always releasing when you least expect it; and c) there is no such thing as pulling the operating rod up, unless you actually wish to strip the rifle.

11. The proper instruments for checking a used or unknown Garand barrel are the throat and muzzle erosion gauges or porcine bullets for the muzzle, which can approximate the data to be gleaned there.

The eyeball, even assisted by optics, can only tell you if something has died there, and there are many charlatans (especially at gun shows) who specialize in polishing and dressing worn out barrels. Many good-looking bores on GI rifles I've checked out gauged 8 or more (virtually unusable) on the TEG. For .308/7.62 rifles, the M14 throat gauge is needed. Civilian barrels of modern design use gentler leades (one of the reasons they last longer) and may gauge 4 or 5 brand new, which is fine. However, what you need to know is this: an M1 bore that one has merely studied with the eye is an orifice about which *nothing* is known.

TROUBLESHOOTING AND GENERAL MAINTENANCE

NOTE: Experienced Garand shooters will note that freshly refinished rifles virtually never release the bolt the instant the clip is latched. For hundreds of rounds, a boosting pat to the operating rod is necessary to drive the first round into the chamber. Sometimes, they will not even eject the clip until worn in.

Many new California-produced clips are available, but their finish is too thick. They seldom function properly until used many times.

IMPORTANT: **NEVER PULL UP ON THE OPERATING ROD WHEN OPENING THE BREECH.** *Pull the operating rod straight back, and straight back only!!!* When you pull up you are asking the operating rod to slip out of the channel, and it will try to obey.

TROUBLESHOOTING AND GENERAL MAINTENANCE

Troubleshooting

Table 4-1. Troubleshooting

Malfunction	Probable cause	Corrective action
	RIFLE M1, M1C (Sniper's) AND M1D (Sniper's)	
Cartridge clip inserts with difficulty.	Deformed clip	Replace.
	Broken ejector	Replace.
	Interference between bullet guide and follower arm.	Replace bullet guide.
Short recoil	Undersized or out of round operating rod piston.	Replace operating rod assembly.
	Oversized gas cylinder	Replace.
	Undersized barrel at gas port	Turn-in weapon for replacement.
	Carbon in gas cylinder	Clean.
	Carbon or foreign matter in gas port of barrel.	Clean.
	Operating rod assembly binding	Replace operating rod assembly if damaged, or relieve wood from gun stock assembly, where operating rod binds on wood.
	Leak in gas cylinder lock screw with valve.	Replace gas cylinder lock screw with valve.
	Defective helical spring (operating rod)	Replace helical spring (operating rod).
	Bolt binding	Remove burs from bolt.
	Distorted or damaged receiver	Repair or turn in for replacement.
Bolt fails to close tightly	Extractor does not open enough to pass over rim of cartridge.	Clean bolt assembly.
	Operating rod assembly binding	Replace operating rod or relieve wood from stock assembly where operating rod binds on wood.
	Weak or broken helical spring (operating rod).	Replace helical spring (operating rod).
	Rust or dirt in chamber	Clean barrel chamber.
	Damaged cartridge, or frozen ejector	Repair or replace ejector.
	Damaged or deformed bolt and/or receiver.	Replace bolt or turn in weapon for replacement.
	Insufficient headspace	Replace bolt assembly by selective fit or turn in weapon for replacement.
Bolt does not release when clip is latched.	Insufficient radii on operating rod catch or operating rod hooks.	Repair or replace operating rod catch or operating rod assembly.
	Bullet guide low at accelerator bearing point.	Replace.
Bolt released before clip is latched.	Worn or broken clip latch.	Replace.
	Worn or broken helical spring (latch)	Replace helical spring (latch).

Troubleshooting guide from US TM 9-1005-222-35 (Source: Dept. of Army, 2/66).

Troubleshooting—Continued

Malfunction	Probable cause	Corrective action
	Excessive radii on operating rod catch or operating rod assembly.	Replace operating rod catch or operating rod assembly.
	Bullet guide high at accelerator bearing point.	Replace.
Bolt fails to be held rearward after firing last round of clip and clip held inside of rifle jammed by bolt.	Bolt does not move sufficiently rearward.	See short recoil.
	Binding latch --------------------	Replace latch.
	Arm or operating rod catch bent or deformed.	Replace operating rod assembly.
Failure to eject cartridge case ---	Low power, causing short recoil	Correct short recoil malfunctions.
	Weak, missing, or frozen helical spring (ejector).	Replace helical spring (ejector).
	Ejector binds--------------------	Clean bolt ejector opening or remove burs from ejector.
	Short recoil --------------------	Clean gas port. Replace operating rod assembly or helical spring.
Failure to eject cartridge clip ---	Clip ejector worn, weak, or broken.	Replace.
	Operating rod catch deformed or broken.	Replace catch.
Failure of bolt to open after firing	Plugged gas port ---------------	Clean.
	Loose gas cylinder-------------	Replace gas cylinder.
	Barrel undersize at gas port area	Turn in weapon for replacement.
	Gas cylinder lock screw with valve fails to close.	Replace.
Failure to fire--------------------	Light indent on primer ---------	Replace helical spring (hammer).
	Inadequate firing pin protrusion	Replace.
	Hammer spring housing damaged	Replace.
Pressure on trigger does not release hammer.	Deformed trigger, pin, or hammer.	Replace defective trigger, pin or hammer.
One or more live cartridges ejected with clip.	Operating rod assembly releases too soon when clip is inserted.	Replace operating rod catch and bullet guide.
Operating rod assembly disengages from bolt while firing.	Worn operating rod lug or kinked helical spring (operating rod assembly).	Replace operating rod assembly or helical spring.

PHOTO 21. "Failure of the bullet guide and/or operating rod catch can lead to the ejection of multiple live rounds, in addition to the spent case and cartridge clip," stated the author after having had just such an experience.

PHOTO 22. Stripping the M1 begins with opening the trigger guard to allow the trigger/hammer group to be removed from the stock and receiver assembly. The spring steel trigger guard, issue on all postwar rifles, is a much superior assembly to the older, heavier "milled" unit, which was easily distorted and allowed no easy readjustment.

TECHNICAL MANUAL

MAINTENANCE

U. S. RIFLE GARAND

Caliber .30 M1

BERETTA ARMS COMPANY - BRESCIA - ITALY

Beretta Arms Co. Technical
Manual: *Maintenance of the
U.S. Rifle Garand Caliber
.30 M1.*

CONTENTS

Page

SECTION I
INTRODUCTION

The U. S. Garand Rifle, caliber .30 M1, is a gas-operated, clip-loaded, air-cooled, semiautomatic shoulder weapon.

There are many features of the Garand M1 Rifle which make it one of the best among all the military semiautomatics. These include reliable functioning, ruggedness, protection of the shooter against gas leaks and blowbacks, excellent appearance, good balance, simplicity and relative fewness of parts, and a short receiver.

It is notable that the M1 rifle has only 82 components, including springs, screws and pins. It is also interesting to note that, in order to insure against premature discharge of the M1 Rifle, the hammer is so constructed that it cannot strike the firing pin before the bolt is rotated into a fully locked position. To provide an added safety measure, the firing pin is prevented from travelling forward until the same condition exists.

The Garand Rifle is probably the easiest to disassemble of any military semiautomatic ever developed. In an instant, it can be separated into three main groups consisting of the stock group, the barrel and receiver group, and the trigger housing group.

A feature of the Garand Rifle which is of interest to any target shooter is the type of the ignition blow applied by the firing pin to the primer.

In most weapons, the firing pin blow is either directly or indirectly caused by a compressed spring and the energy in the spring usually decreases as the firing pin moves forward. Thus, when the spring becomes fatigued, the impact on the primer is materially reduced and the result may be hangfires or misfires. In the Garand firing mechanism, the construction which controls the hammer is such that the leverage is increased as the hammer nears the point of impact, which tends to reduce the load on the sear, cause the trigger to pull easily, and increase the load on the firing pin at the time of firing, helping to prevent the extrusion of the primer into the firing pin hole. Another point of interest is the lock time; that is, the time required from the moment the trigger is pulled until the moment the firing pin impinges on the primer. In the Garand Rifle, this has been designed to be just. 0057 second.

1

SECTION II
MEASUREMENTS AND DATA

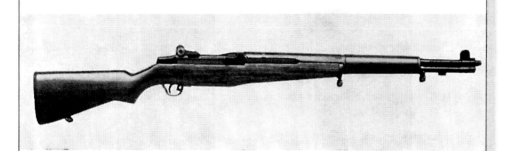

Caliber: .30 U. S.

Weight: 9.5 lbs. (The density of the wood in the stock varies from one gun to the next, changing the weight slightly).

Length (over-all) Rifle Only: 43.6 in.

Length (over-all) With Bayonet: 53.4 in.

Length of Barrel: 24 in.

Length of Rifling: 21.30 in.

Rifling:

   Right-Hand Twist: 1 turn in 10 in.

   Depth of Grooves: 0.0040 in.

Cross-Sectional Area of Bore: 0.0740 sq. in.

Type of Mechanism: Gas-Operated, Semiautomatic.

Magazine: Fixed box type in receiver loaded with clip.

Cartridge Clip: Capacity 8 rounds, clip is inserted in the Rifle with the cartridges.

Wen Last Shot Has Been Fired: Empty cartridge clip is expelled through top of the Rifle.

Rate of Fire: Semiautomatic.

Sights: Aperture, adjustable from 100 to 1200 yards.

Sight Radius: 27.9 in. at 100 yard range.

Trigger Pull: 7.5 lbs. max., 5.5 lbs. min.

Normal Pressure: 50,000 lbs. per sq. in.

Approximate Maximum Range: 3,450 yards.

Locking: By rotating bolt with two lugs which fit into recess in the receiver.

Ejection: Empty cartridge cases are ejected on the right, upwards and to the front. When rifle is empty, bolt will stay open. This serves notice that the weapon is empty and permits immediate insertion of a fully loaded clip, so that firing may be speedily resumed.

2

SECTION III
LOADING, FIRING AND UNLOADING

Loading and Firing

1. Grasping the rifle at the balance with the left hand; with the right fore-finger, pull operating rod straight to the rear. It will be caught and held open by the operating rod catch.

2. Place the loaded clip on top of the magazine follower and, with right side of right hand against the operating rod handle, press down with right thumb on the clip, until it is caught in the receiver by the clip latch.

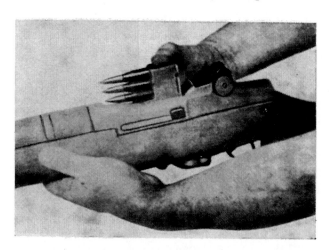

3. Remove the right thumb from the line of the bolt and let go on the operating rod handle, which will run forward under the pression of the spring. Push operating rod handle with heel of right hand to be sure that bolt is fully home and locked.

4. Pressing the trigger will now fire one cartridge. Weapon will be ready for the next pull of the trigger.

5. If weapon is not to be used at once, set the safety. The safety is in front of the trigger guard. Pulling it back towards the trigger sets it on safe, while pushing it forward is the fire position.
Note that the cartridge clip is reversible and may be fed into the rifle from either end.

3

Unloading the Garand Rifle

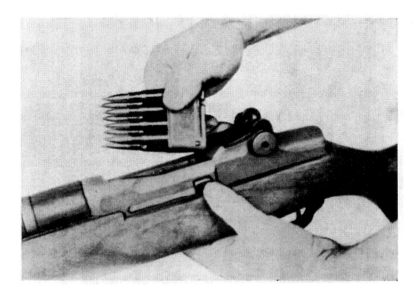

1. First check to be sure that the safety is set.

2. With the right forefinger, pull the operating rod back sharply and hold it in the rear position. This will eject the cartridge that was in the firing chamber. With the fingers of the hand grasp the trigger guard or the grip firmly. Hold the stock against the right hip to support it. Then place the left hand over the receiver and, with the left thumb, release the clip latch.

3. The clip and whatever cartridges remain in it will now pop up into the right hand and must be removed from the rifle.

4. With the right side of the right hand held against the operating rod handle, force the operating rod slightly to the rear. With the right thumb now push down the magazine follower and permit the bolt to move forward about an inch over the end of the follower.

5. Remove the thumb smartly from the follower and let go on the operating rod. The action will close under the tension of the spring. Now press the trigger.

4

SECTION IV
FIELD STRIPPING

To Dismount Stock Group

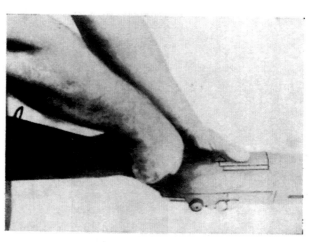

1. Start by placing the rifle upside down on a firm surface. Holding the rifle with left hand, finger firmly holding the base of the trigger housing, rest the butt against the left thigh.

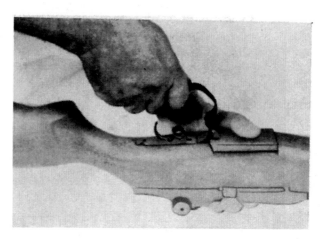

2. With thumb and forefinger unlatch the trigger guard by pulling back on it.

5

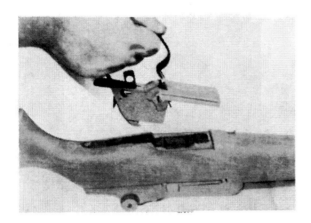

3. Continue the pressure and pull out the trigger housing group.

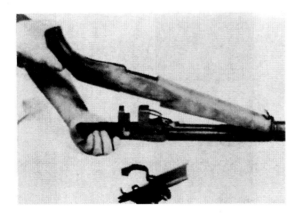

4. With left hand now grasp rifle over rear sight, holding the muzzle down and the barrel to your left.

With right hand strike down against the small of the stock, firmly grasping it at the same time.

This will separate the barrel and receiver group from the stock group.

6

To Dismount Barrel and Receiver Group

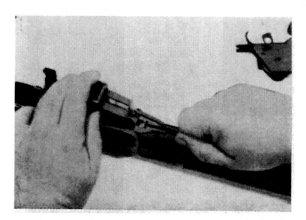

1. With the barrel down, grasp the follower rod with thumb and forefinger and press it toward the muzzle to free it from the follower arm.

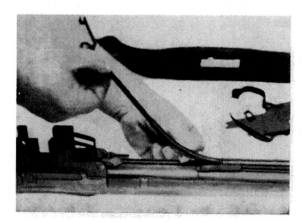

2. The follower rod and its compensating spring which is attached may now be withdrawn to the right. The compensating spring is removed from the follower rod by holding spring with left hand twisting rod toward the body with the right hand, meanwhile pulling slightly to the right.

7

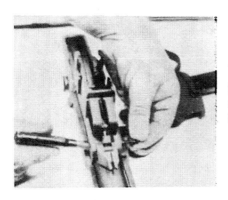

3. With the point of a bullet, push the follower arm pin from its seat and pull it out with the left hand.

4. Seize the bullet guide, follower arm and operating rod catch assembly; pull these up until they disengage. The three separate parts may now be lifted out. Accelerator pin is riveted in its seat, so do not attempt to remove accelerator from operating catch assembly.

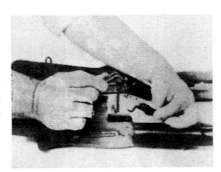

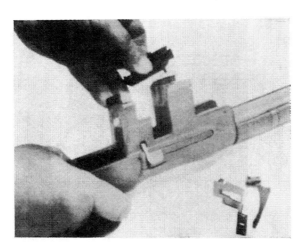

5. Lift out follower with its slide attached (do not separate follower from slide).

8

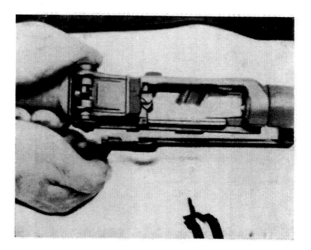

6. Holding barrel and receiver assembly with left hand, grasp the operating rod handle with rigth hand and move it slightly to the rear, meanwhile pulling the rod handle up and away from the receiver. (This disengages operating rod from bolt, when the lug on the operating rod slides into the dismount notch of the operating rod guide groove).

When operating rod is disengaged pull it down and back and withdraw it. (Note that the operating rod is bent. This is intentional. Do not attempt to straighten it).

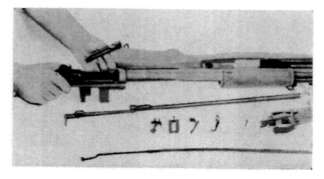

7. Slide the bolt from the rear to the front by pushing the operating lug on it and lift it out to the right front with a slight twisting motion.

9

To Dismount Gas Cylinder

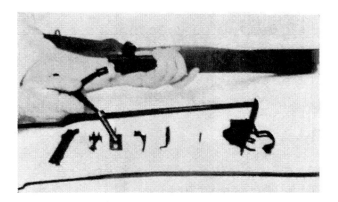

1. The combination tool is used to unscrew the gas cylinder lock screw.

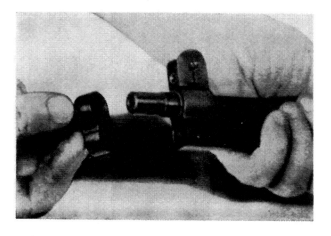

2. Next the gas cylinder lock is unscrewed.

10

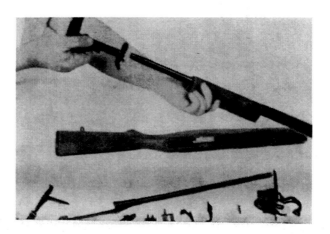

3. The gas cylinder is tapped toward the muzzle and removed from the barrel. The front sight is not to be dismounted from gas cylinder assembly.

4. Gas cylinder assembly should never be removed except when necessary to replace the front hand guard assembly.

11

SECTION V
ASSEMBLING

1. Replacing gas cylinder, if it has been dismounted, is done by merely reversing the dismounting procedure.

2. To assemble barrel and receiver group: tilt the barrel and receiver assembly, sight up and muzzle to the front to an angle of about 45°.

3. Holding the bolt by the right locking lug so the front end of the bolt is somewhat above and to the right of its extreme forward position in the receiver, insert the rear end in its bearing on the bridge of the receiver. Switch it from right to left far enough to let tang of the firing pin clear to the top of the bridge. Next, guide the left locking lug of the bolt into its groove just to the rear of the lug on the left side of the receiver and start right locking lug into its bearing in the receiver. Now slide bolt back to its extreme rear position.

4. Turn barrel and receiver assembly in the left hand until barrel is down.

5 Grasp operating rod at the handle holding it handle up, insert piston head into gas cylinder about 3/8". Be sure that operating rod handle is to the left of the receiver.

6. Hold barrel and receiver assembly in the left hand and twist to the right until barrel is uppermost.

7. Adjust operating rod with right hand so that camming recess on its rear end fits over operating lug on bolt. Now press operating rod forward and downward until bolt is seated in its forward position.

8. With barrel and receiver assembly held barrel down and muzzle to your left, replace the follower with its attached slide so that its guide ribs fit into their grooves in the receiver. The follower slide rests on the bottom surface of the bolt when the follower is in the correct position.

9. With left hand replace bullet guide fitting the shoulders of the guide into their slots in the receiver and the hole in the projecting lug is in line with the hole in the receiver.

10. With left hand, replace follower arm passing stud end through bullet guide slot and inserting stud in proper grooves in front end of follower.

11. Place the forked end of the follower arm in position across the projecting lug on the bullet guide, with pin holes properly alined.

12

12. Insert rear arm of operating rod catch into clearance cut in the bullet guide (be sure its rear end is below the forward stud of the clip latch which projects into the receiver mouth). Line up the holes in the operating rod catch, the follower arm and the bullet guide with those in the receiver and insert the follower arm pin in the side of the receiver towards your body, pressing the pin home.

13. Insert operating rod spring into operating rod and assemble follower rod by grasping the spring in the left hand and inserting follower rod with right hand, then twisting the two together until the spring is fully seated.

14. Seize the follower rod with thumb and forefinger of left hand with hump down and forked end to the right.

15. Place front end of follower rod into operating rod spring and push to the left, seating the forked end against the follower arm.

16. Insert U shaped flange of stock ferrule in its seat in the lower band.

17. Pivoting about this group, guide chamber and receiver group and press into position in the stock.

18. Replace trigger housing group with trigger guard in open position into the stock opening.

19. Press into position, close and latch trigger guard. This completes reassembling.

13

SECTION VI
FUNCTIONING

Starting with the rifle loaded and cocked, the action is as follows: The trigger being pressed, the hammer strikes the firing pin, exploding the cartridge in the chamber. As the bullet passes over the gas port drilled in the under side of the barrel, some of the gas escapes into the cylinder and blasts back against the piston and operating rod with strength enough to drive the rod to the rear and compress the return spring.

During the first 5/16" of the rearward travel, the operating lug slides in a straight section of the recess on the operating rod, after which the cam surface of this recess is brought in contact with the operating lug which it cams up, thereby rotating the bolt from right to left to unlock its two lugs from their recesses in the receiver.

During the moment of delayed action, the bullet leaves the barrel and the breech pressure drops to a safe point. The further rotation of the bolt then cams the hammer away from the firing pin and pulls the firing pin back from the bolt. The operating rod continues its backward movement carrying the bolt with it as the lug on the bolt has reached the end of its recess.
During this rearward motion of the bolt, the empty case is withdrawn from the chamber by the extractor positioned in the bolt until it is clear of the breech; at which point the ejector, exerting a steady pressure on the base of the cartridge case, throws it to the right front by the action of its compressed spring.

The rear end of the bolt at this point forces the hammer back, rides over it and compresses the hammer spring; finally it stops in the rear end of the receiver.

As the bolt has now cleared the clip, the follower spring forces the cartridge up until the topmost one is in line with the bolt.

The operating rod spring comes into play at this point to pull the action forward.

Forward Movement of the Action: As the bolt moves forward, its lower front base strikes the base of the cartridge case and pushes it into the firing chamber. The hammer, pressed by its spring, rides on the bottom of the bolt. While it tends to rise, it is caught and held by the trigger lugs engaging the

14

hammer-hook, if trigger pressure has been released. Otherwise, the trigger engages the rear hammer hook until letting go the trigger disengages the scar from the hammer. The hammer then slides into engagement with the trigger lugs.

When the bolt nears its forward position, the extractor engages near the rim of the cartridge and the base of the cartridge forces the ejector into the bolt, compressing the ejector spring.

The rear surface of the cam recess in the operating rod now cams the operating lug down and thereby twists the bolt from left to right until the two lugs lock into their places in the receiver.

The operating rod drives ahead for another 5/16". The rear end of the straight section of the operating rod recess reaches the operating lug on the bolt, which completes the forward movement and leaves the rifle ready to fire when the trigger is pressed.

This cycle continues as long as there are any cartridges in the magazine and the trigger is squeezed.

15

50

SECTION VII
CARE OF THE RIFLE

The rifle must be kept clean and properly lubricated. Failure to do so may result in stoppages at a critical moment. The rifle is to be inspected periodically.

To Clean the Bore: A clean patch saturated with hot water and soap should be run through the bore a number of times. While the bore is still wet, a metal brush should be run through several times to loosen up any material which has not been dissolved by the water. Dry patches should then be pushed through the bore until thoroughly dry. The bore should then be coated with light issue of gun oil. Also use the chamber cleaning tool to give the chamber the same attention. Remember that powder fouling in the bore contains a salt which rusts the steel.

To Clean Gas Cylinder: The carbon must be scraped from the exposed surfaces, the front of the cylinder and the gas cylinder plug and piston head, after extensive fire. The mess kit knife or similar sharp bladed instruments should be used for this scraping process. Gas cylinder plugs and grooves in the gas cylinder should be cleaned so they will feed correctly in the plug.

Attention to other Parts of Rifle: Graphite cup grease is excellent for lubricating bolt lugs, bolt guides, bolt cocking cams, compensating spring, contact surfaces of barrel and operating rod, operating rod cams and springs, and operating rod groove in the receiver.

All other metal parts should be cleaned and covered with a uniform light coat of oil.

Rust should be removed from the metal parts with a piece of soft wood and oil, never with abrasive. Screw heads must be kept clean to prevent rusting.

Be careful not to use too much oil as any heavy coat will collect dirt and interfere with operations.

16

PIETRO BERETTA S. p. A.

The Foremost Italian Manufacturer
of Shotguns, Pistols, Rifles
and Lightweight Weapons

Gardone V.T. - Brescia
Italy

NATIONAL MATCH, ACCURACY RIFLES

The purpose of the National Match or competition Garand is to hit reliably at ranges that may reach as deep as 1,000 meters, and to do so in strings of fire involving a maximum of 20 rounds expended at a sitting.

This section contains data, photos, and illustrations relating to the M1 Garand's preparation as an accuracy rifle. The military text reproduced at the end of Part II is on the Rifle, National Match, M1 and was released by the U.S. Army Material Command/Weapons Command at Camp Perry in 1963. It is obsolete, and no one today contemplating the best possible competition rifle seriously considers a military barrel. However, it does lay out excellent assembly and test procedures, and, though modern materials are much improved, every bit of practical information in the manual is useful.

Most civilian shooters will not bother with the marking procedures detailed in the text. Line and tension straightening barrels should never be necessary any more. The procedure is sometimes done by manufacturers before delivery, but with today's broaching techniques and button rifling, the term itself has fallen into disuse and has become obsolete.

Likewise, the suggestion that cleaning the bore after firing is unnecessary has been known to be false since long before this literature was prepared. Removal of copper fouling in particular, especially after extensive shooting of a rapid-fire rifle with fast-moving bullets, has been proven many thousands—probably millions—of times, to be an absolute *necessity* for both barrel life and best shooting. One will still

PHOTO 23. Many latter-day M1 Garand accuracy rifles, especially those used for long-range shooting, feature modified, relieved gas systems—variable versions of the old "solid" gas cylinder lock screw (plug) designed to vent some high-pressure gas when high-pressure, long-range loads are employed. This one, from Derrick Martin of Accuracy Speaks in Mesa, Arizona, can be very advantageous with the heavier bullets at 500 yards and beyond.

JUST AS this book goes to press, yet another project is under way that might prolong the life of at least one specimen of the paramount rifle of the 1940s into a great rifle of the 21st century. Actually, it's a two-part experiment whose goal, quite simply, is to preserve a Garand and especially, its barrel for a very long time. Ant it's technology that is not brutally expensive.

Cryo treatment involves immersing metal products subject to high stress into a tank of liquid nitrogen at temperatures fairly close to absolute zero, then precisely returning the assembly to normal temperature ranges. This is similar to heat treatment but has little or no impact on Rockwell hardness. It does, however, improve molecular cohesion at a near-atomic level, meaning metals so treated are far less subject to microfracture and fatigue.

Molycoating bullets involves using a complex polymer, coated with a high-temperature variant of Carnuba wax, in a special tumbler. Its primary effect is to minimize the shedding of copper, which tends to gall onto barrel steel. For now, this process is available and of use only to handloaders, though surely someone will find a way to market the processed bullets, loaded, to casual shooters of loaded ammo.

Between the two processes, it may now be possible to prolong the life of the Garand—especially its barrel, bolt, and operating rod—and to minimize the effects of heat and copper fouling on Garand barrels.

Unlike a lot of "panacea" mumbo-jumbo of the past, these two processes have real history and real impact . . . . The question that will be explored is how much impact? Stay tuned . . .

sometimes encounter some walking antique at a rifle range who suggests that cleaning a match rifle is somehow an error. This "logic" is as erroneous and tortured as the statement itself.

However, the admonition that detailed disassembly of a tightly bedded rifle is both difficult and, in some ways, counterproductive *is* at least partially correct. Upon reassembly, such a rifle will require six to eight rounds to seat properly back into the bedding, and zero may shift slight-

PHOTO 24. Most depot-built and some arsenal competition rifles, when actually in service, acquired a lot of local markings and even painted bands, largely to discourage theft.

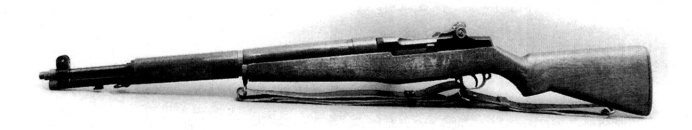

PHOTO 25. This 7.62mm USMC Match gun was apparently prepared for demonstration use at Quantico and features a great many hard chrome and black chromed or oxided parts and a Douglas barrel with full local markings.

PHOTO 26. Properly set up, the ejector on the Garand will dump .308/7.62mm brass neatly and consistently where a shooter can find it quickly and efficiently. This H&R bears a custom barrel, and the bolt and ejector have received a great deal of detailed attention, which saves a great deal of time at the range and contributes to both accuracy and reliability. Rounds from this rifle land, reliably, about 3 feet in front of the rifle, perhaps a foot to the right.

PHOTO 27. There were many stages in the evolution of the fine adjustment National Match sight, including the "small tin can" hooded version, shown elsewhere in this book, from the 1950s. Here are the standard H&R service sight, ca. 1955; the rare first model small aperture National Match, ca. 1949; and a typical Winchester aperture from about 1942, for comparison, from left to right.

ly. So the procedure for cleaning the gas system without total disassembly becomes very important. Lubrication with more modern greases than were in military use in 1963 becomes much more important with match rifles because accessing the operating rod and spring is so awkward.

There were depot-prepared match Garands—and, likely, considerable activity at Springfield Armory as well—long after 1963. Indeed, many of the navy's wonderful 7.62mm match rifles seem to have been rebuilt and reconfigured at H&R, apparently well into the 1970s.

One factor the military very thoroughly explored, which I regard as more or less gospel, is the curious inter-relationship between bullets and velocity for achieving maximum accuracy. Work done at Frankford Arsenal, Aberdeen, and Lake City led to conclusions that I tried for a long time to disprove and that I and every other serious researcher I know can only affirm: *bullets of a given weight and design, virtually regardless of the type or brand of powder, will deliver best accuracy at a very specific velocity level.* This is nothing new, but every handloader and many manufacturers keep trying to change this fundamental principle, with very limited success. *This is not to say that your pet load is not at least partially dependent on the type and quantity of powder you use.* What it does state, though, is that optimal performance appears at certain specific velocity "windows," even if different cartridges are used. In this case, of course, we're discussing 7.62mm (.308 diameter, or .30 caliber) virtually exclusively.

cont'd. on page 57

That said, I have noticed (and have spent *ungodly* amounts of powder working out this data) that there is far less difference in accuracy potential—given the use of any medium-slow rifle powder appropriate for this rifle and these cartridges—than some authorities would have you believe. I have gotten roughly equal results from carefully worked-up loads in .30/06 and .308 with Varget, IMR 4064, both versions of 4895, Winchester's 748 and 760 ball, and at least a dozen others, some mentioned in other parts of this book.

The velocity "peaks" in the match barrels and high-quality GI barrels I've shot run about as follows:

BULLET AND TYPE	VELOCITY OPTIMUM "WINDOW" *
147-152 grain service-style ball USGI, PMC, Israeli, Winchester, commercial, flatbase or boat-tail—though flatbases actually have slightly less muzzle velocity latitude and are slightly more individual	approx. 2,690-2,810 fps
168-175 grain FMJ boat-tail match bullets, hollowpoints and other	approx. 2,590-2,660 fps
180-190 grain boat-tail hollowpoint match	approx. 2,400-2,540 fps

Note: Some long-range shooters push much faster and make special gas cylinder changes to shoot such rounds in the Garand. Do not do this in any standard rifle.

*These figures are all muzzle velocities.

For all the practical reasons noted elsewhere in this book, it is strongly suggested that today's match conversions of the Garand be executed in 7.62x51/.308.

Wise Garand shooters will polish the ejector and, especially, the knife edge of the extractor. Snipping a couple of coils off the ejector spring will keep one's spent brass closer to shooting position, and in better condition. These modifications will reduce ejector "hickeyes" on caseheads. The Garand was designed so that casings landed far away from the rifle to minimize clutter in static combat positions. You're not likely to require that dispersion.

Presuming a receiver is not excessively worn, particularly in the operating rod raceway (and is hopefully a late World War II or post-war unit), there is no reason a properly prepared Garand with top-quality ammo cannot easily exceed minute-of-angle accuracy with regularity. Sometimes this can happen with far less than full match preparation. The barrel, of course, is critical to this formula. Whether a receiver has spent part of its life in a foreign country is irrelevant. (Regardless of who the last military owner was, virtually every M1 has seen service abroad, a very high percentage even of DCM rifles having been foreign-owned at some time or other.) *All* of the very best shooting M1s I've fired were civilian workups on import receivers. In fact, entering competition with an arsenal "NM" rifle is a certain way to carefully avoid victory.

It is much better to begin anew and make use of some of the discoveries of the last 30 or so years.

Just as important to note is that an actual, certifiable GI SA NM rifle is an artifact. For half its value to a collector, a much better custom rifle can be concocted with brand new heavy Fajen stock and Douglas barrel.

The GI bedding specifications for the receiver are rather conservative. Most modern smiths put an "S" layer of hard bedding or even a steel "reclining L" piece at the receiver's foremost left corner wedge, ahead of the clip release, about 1 inch behind and below the receiver ring. Some also weld or bolt a heavy square wedge below the receiver "horseshoe" and inlet this into another bedded well in the buttstock. This increases bearing area and, in theory, stability—although with this robust receiver it may be unnecessary. Most smiths fiddle the stock ferrule around to provide a high level of upward spring tension to hold the barrel high. This is very helpful as the gun heats up. Springfield never did these procedures; nor was its bedding very secure.

Modern barrel crowns are less exaggerated and less fragile than 30-odd years back. One of the best ideas I've seen was on a custom-turned barrel, some 1/8 inch of which was belled out and slightly countersunk. This shooter cleaned at the firing line with copper solvent—rapidly, at every opportunity—and was shooting scores way above his level of experience.

By the way, if you have some old USGI 173 grain M72 bullets, the original form of the manual makes very clear that their optimum specific velocity level (at the muzzle, of course) was 2,640 fps., which neatly fits my research parameters.

There's a certain amount of pedantics, nostalgia, and romance associated with this old rifle, and I don't object to any of it. Indeed, I celebrate it. However, to me, the best way to celebrate this legend is to neatly plop bullets into paper, way downrange, one on top of the other. Good luck—and good shooting!

cleaning effort and time. Velocity increases per load are very minimal; I saw no accuracy increase whatever. But for the price per bullet, the increase in barrel life is very sensible. All testing was done with 175-grain Hornady boat-tail hollow-point match bullets. The factories do not as yet apply this process to *any* of their ammunition. Some factory ammunition utilizes other polymer coatings. The "molycoating" may be applied to any caliber, and by the time you read this, *all* of my bullets will be so prepared.

The third development is also nothing really new but has been receiving a lot of attention lately; processes have improved, and prices for application are, correspondingly, decreasing. Cryogenic tempering subjects objects to temperatures below -300 degrees Fahrenheit for precisely controlled time intervals. Structure, stress, and crystalline arrangement are subtly modified, depending upon the material. The exposure to liquid nitrogen temperatures of this order sometimes eliminates specific accuracy problems related to tool stress and, with many materials, can greatly increase wear resistance. It has little to no effect upon the 8620 tool steel of the Garand's receiver but should significantly increase the life of most M1 barrels, particularly those which evince stress "bends" from machining processes. *Guns and Ammo* and *American Rifleman*, among others, have run fairly detailed features on the processes and results.

Cryogenic processing seems to add considerable life to most barrel steels. It can increase accuracy, though usually with near-new barrels that have experienced machin-

cont'd. on page 58

• • • • •

ing stress (this sort of stress cannot usually be relieved with older techniques). The processes are not expensive, and my examination of M1 barrels thus prepared has so far indicated that the cryogenic treatment very slightly decreases cleaning time but considerably slows fatigue and throat burn.

All three can be good news to Garand shooters, and even to collectors.

This manual dates from long before Kevlar-augmented epoxy bedding, laser-measured barrels, and some of the more radical techniques successfully used by America's best riflesmiths to build the best high-powered competition rifles in the country.

Despite the ravings of various hacks in the political realm, the M1 has never been popular with thugs, but its rapid-fire capability has made it one of the darlings of the competition firing line. Its offspring, the M14 and various cast copies, carry 20-round magazines and have some advantage in the longer, timed strings, but are not as strong. Smith's semiautomatic M14, among others, is in the same accuracy class as the M1. The M14 was included in the original version of this manual but has been deleted in this excerpt.

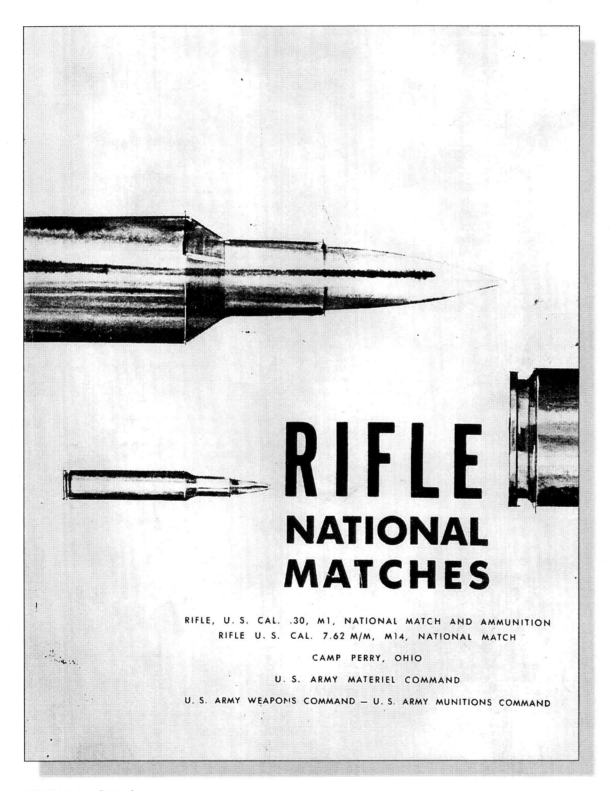

RIFLE, National Matches.

RIFLE, U. S., CAL. .30, M1, NATIONAL MATCH

PART I — HISTORY

1. In March, 1953, Springfield Armory was directed by Office, Chief of Ordnance to furnish 800 U. S. Cal. .30 M1, Rifles for use at the National Matches. These rifles were to be selected as being of excellent quality and workmanship and should possess accuracy (size of groups), and targeting (location of group), capabilities superior to the average service weapon. The Armory, at that time, was manufacturing new M1 rifles, a situation which naturally lessened the work required to produce the desired lot of match quality guns. Because of the high standards to which the service rifles were being produced it was necessary to apply only minor gunsmithing to any weapon to obtain National Match quality.

2. During the succeeding years from 1954 through 1963 the Armory produced National Match quality weapons by two methods, namely; (1) by applying minor gunsmithing operations to newly manufactured rifles as described in the preceding paragraph and (2) by rebuilding National Match weapons returned to the installation from various locations throughout the world. The latter procedure requires a considerable amount of inspection, refinishing, and rebuilding of weapon components. This work is necessary to eliminate parts which evidence excessive wear or which have been altered in the field for some particular reason. Each rebuilt National Match rifle is rebarreled, restocked and glass bedded.

3. Inasmuch as production of new Cal. .30 M1 Rifles has been completely curtailed, M1, NM Rifles to be issued during the 1963 National Matches are rebuilt weapons. However, because of the critical acceptance standards applicable to National Match rifles, and because of the expert workmanship employed to meet these standards it is not likely the user will be able to distinguish between new and rebuilt weapons either in appearance or performance.

4. The following year by year breakdown indicates the quantity of National Match Cal. .30 M1 rifles produced by Springfield Armory:

Year	New	Rebuilt	Total
1953	800		800
1954	4184	499	4683
1955	3003	314	3317
1956	5050	550	5600
1957	4184	499	4683
1958	1295	731	2026
1959	2877	2652	5529
1960		8663	8663
1961		1410	1410
1962		4500	4500
1963		3639	3639

PART II — 1963 RIFLE

The 1963 model shown above represents the latest refinement of the M1 as a National Match rifle.

Over the years many modifications have been made to improve the accuracy and targeting capabilities of the M1. Those described on page 3 and illustrated on pages 4 and 5 have been found to produce the best results when judged by the performance average of large numbers of rifles.

This year's National Match M1 has a hooded eyepiece rear sight. This sight will make possible ½ minute changes in elevation, and will be available in two peep hole diameters. Scores will improve with the hooded eyepiece as the sight picture will be much more constant under changing light conditions.

In addition, new rear sight bases have been modified to considerably minimize movement between the aperture assembly and the mating surfaces in the base. The new rear sight base will be identified with the letters NM/2A.

The new hooded rear sight is shown on page 6. Operation of the sight, firing mechanism, and other points of interest are described on pages 7, 8 and 9.

Notes on inspection of barrels and of the completed rifle will be found in Part IV. Part V will provide useful information on rifle maintenance.

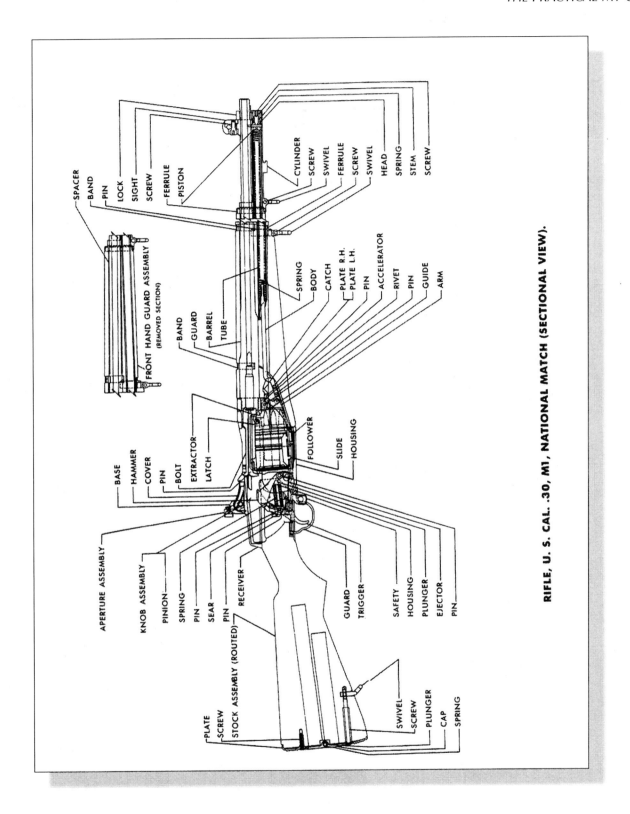

RIFLE, U. S. CAL. .30, M1, NATIONAL MATCH (SECTIONAL VIEW).

PART III — GENERAL REQUIREMENTS

1. All components shall be of latest design.

2. All wooden components shall be of solid heartwood with the direction of grain parallel to the longitudinal axis of stock.

3. All stocks shall be glass bedded and custom fitted to receiver and barrel assemblies and trigger housing assemblies. The stock assembly and the trigger housing assembly shall be identified with last four digits of the receiver serial number. These assemblies shall not be interchanged after glass bedding process has been completed.

4. The stock shall be free from contact with the barrel or handguard.

5. Stock ferrule shall not contact lower portion of lower band longitudinally; there shall be approximately 1/64 inch minimum clearance.

6. The stock shall have a clearance in the area between rear of receiver bedding surface and receiver rail bedding surfaces.

7. Clamping of the trigger guard shall have a definite resistance at a minimum distance of ⅜ inch from the full lock position.

8. Gas cylinder shall fit tightly on the barrel bearing diameter and the splines. There shall be no rotational movement.

9. Gas cylinder shall be brought forward against the lock before tightening the gas cylinder lock screw.

10. In assembly, the gas cylinder lock shall be hand tightened against shoulder on the barrel within a range of slightly beyond the 6 o'clock position but not in excess of 60° (8 o'clock) past the 6 o'clock position. The gas cylinder lock shall then be "backed off" the minimum distance necessary to align with the gas cylinder at the 6 o'clock position.

11. Gas cylinder splined hole and rear ring shall meet requirements of alignment gage.

12. The barrel muzzle shall be crowned — concentric with bore (60° included angle) to remove burrs.

13. The barrel shall be line straightened to meet the requirements of an optical straightness gage. Straightness of the barrel shall be such that the bore centerline established by a self-aligning expansion plug (2½ inches long with a pilot diameter of .2993 minus .0001) that fits and aligns itself in the bore at the muzzle end, the maximum allowable deviation from that centerline shall not exceed 0° 2' 23" throughout the length of the bore. Any resultant taper of the bore shall be within dimensional limits and be diminishing from breech to muzzle.

14. The operating rod assembly shall function freely without binding during a simulated firing cycle with the operating rod spring removed.

15. The trigger pull required to release the hammer shall be smooth, free from "creep," and within the limits of four and one-half to six pounds. Functional surfaces of the hooks of the hammer and trigger, and the related mating surfaces of the sear may have the phosphate coating removed by polishing to assure smooth trigger pull.

16. Aperture assemblies 7791133 and 7791282 produce ½ minute change of elevation by 180° rotation of the aperture. Aperture assembly 7791133 shall have an eyepiece with an .0595 peep hole. Aperture assembly 7791282 shall have an eyepiece with an .0520 peep hole.

17. Threads on windage knob shall measure 5/16-64 NS-3A. Threads on rear sight base shall measure 5/16-64 NS-3B.

18. Top of front sight blade shall be square with side and all edges and corners shall be sharp to .005 R. Max. Front sight shall be sharp and square and shall not overhang the sides of the gas cylinder.

19. Headspace shall be 1.940 to 1.943. Light finger pressure shall be used in checking headspace.

20. Identification mark shall consist of the letters "NM" approximately ⅛ inch high inscribed on the barrel approximately between the front hand guard and front sight.

1. ESSENTIAL POINTS AND AREAS

The essential points and areas established by these general requirements are illustrated on pages 4 and 5.

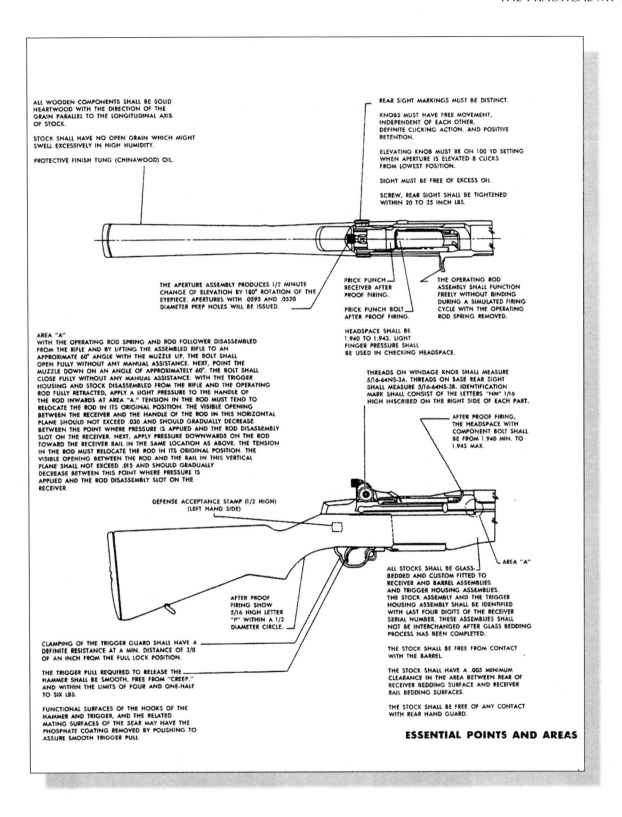

ALL WOODEN COMPONENTS SHALL BE SOLID HEARTWOOD WITH THE DIRECTION OF THE GRAIN PARALLEL TO THE LONGITUDINAL AXIS OF STOCK.

STOCK SHALL HAVE NO OPEN GRAIN WHICH MIGHT SWELL EXCESSIVELY IN HIGH HUMIDITY.

PROTECTIVE FINISH TUNG (CHINAWOOD) OIL.

REAR SIGHT MARKINGS MUST BE DISTINCT.

KNOBS MUST HAVE FREE MOVEMENT, INDEPENDENT OF EACH OTHER, DEFINITE CLICKING ACTION, AND POSITIVE RETENTION.

ELEVATING KNOB MUST BE ON 100 YD SETTING WHEN APERTURE IS ELEVATED 8 CLICKS FROM LOWEST POSITION.

SIGHT MUST BE FREE OF EXCESS OIL.

SCREW, REAR SIGHT SHALL BE TIGHTENED WITHIN 20 TO 25 INCH LBS.

THE APERTURE ASSEMBLY PRODUCES 1/2 MINUTE CHANGE OF ELEVATION BY 180° ROTATION OF THE EYEPIECE. APERTURES WITH .0595 AND .0520 DIAMETER PEEP HOLES WILL BE ISSUED.

PRICK PUNCH RECEIVER AFTER PROOF FIRING.

PRICK PUNCH BOLT AFTER PROOF FIRING.

THE OPERATING ROD ASSEMBLY SHALL FUNCTION FREELY WITHOUT BINDING DURING A SIMULATED FIRING CYCLE WITH THE OPERATING ROD SPRING REMOVED.

HEADSPACE SHALL BE 1.940 TO 1.943. LIGHT FINGER PRESSURE SHALL BE USED IN CHECKING HEADSPACE.

AREA "A"
WITH THE OPERATING ROD SPRING AND ROD FOLLOWER DISASSEMBLED FROM THE RIFLE AND BY LIFTING THE ASSEMBLED RIFLE TO AN APPROXIMATE 60° ANGLE WITH THE MUZZLE UP, THE BOLT SHALL OPEN FULLY WITHOUT ANY MANUAL ASSISTANCE. NEXT, POINT THE MUZZLE DOWN ON AN ANGLE OF APPROXIMATELY 60°. THE BOLT SHALL CLOSE FULLY WITHOUT ANY MANUAL ASSISTANCE. WITH THE TRIGGER HOUSING AND STOCK DISASSEMBLED FROM THE RIFLE AND THE OPERATING ROD FULLY RETRACTED, APPLY A LIGHT PRESSURE TO THE HANDLE OF THE ROD INWARDS AT AREA "A." TENSION IN THE ROD MUST TEND TO RELOCATE THE ROD IN ITS ORIGINAL POSITION. THE VISIBLE OPENING BETWEEN THE RECEIVER AND THE HANDLE OF THE ROD IN THIS HORIZONTAL PLANE SHOULD NOT EXCEED .030 AND SHOULD GRADUALLY DECREASE BETWEEN THE POINT WHERE PRESSURE IS APPLIED AND THE ROD DISASSEMBLY SLOT ON THE RECEIVER. NEXT, APPLY PRESSURE DOWNWARDS ON THE ROD TOWARD THE RECEIVER RAIL IN THE SAME LOCATION AS ABOVE. THE TENSION IN THE ROD MUST RELOCATE THE ROD IN ITS ORIGINAL POSITION. THE VISIBLE OPENING BETWEEN THE ROD AND THE RAIL IN THIS VERTICAL PLANE SHALL NOT EXCEED .015 AND SHOULD GRADUALLY DECREASE BETWEEN THIS POINT WHERE PRESSURE IS APPLIED AND THE ROD DISASSEMBLY SLOT ON THE RECEIVER.

THREADS ON WINDAGE KNOB SHALL MEASURE 5/16-64NS-3A. THREADS ON BASE REAR SIGHT SHALL MEASURE 5/16-64NS-3B. IDENTIFICATION MARK SHALL CONSIST OF THE LETTERS "NM" 1/16 HIGH INSCRIBED ON THE RIGHT SIDE OF EACH PART.

AFTER PROOF FIRING, THE HEADSPACE WITH COMPONENT BOLT SHALL BE FROM 1.940 MIN. TO 1.943 MAX.

DEFENSE ACCEPTANCE STAMP (1/2 HIGH) (LEFT HAND SIDE)

AREA "A"

ALL STOCKS SHALL BE GLASS-BEDDED AND CUSTOM FITTED TO RECEIVER AND BARREL ASSEMBLIES AND TRIGGER HOUSING ASSEMBLIES. THE STOCK ASSEMBLY AND THE TRIGGER HOUSING ASSEMBLY SHALL BE IDENTIFIED WITH LAST FOUR DIGITS OF THE RECEIVER SERIAL NUMBER. THESE ASSEMBLIES SHALL NOT BE INTERCHANGED AFTER GLASS BEDDING PROCESS HAS BEEN COMPLETED.

THE STOCK SHALL BE FREE FROM CONTACT WITH THE BARREL.

THE STOCK SHALL HAVE A .005 MINIMUM CLEARANCE IN THE AREA BETWEEN REAR OF RECEIVER BEDDING SURFACE AND RECEIVER RAIL BEDDING SURFACES.

THE STOCK SHALL BE FREE OF ANY CONTACT WITH REAR HAND GUARD.

AFTER PROOF FIRING SHOW 5/16 HIGH LETTER "P" WITHIN A 1/2 DIAMETER CIRCLE.

CLAMPING OF THE TRIGGER GUARD SHALL HAVE A DEFINITE RESISTANCE AT A MIN. DISTANCE OF 3/8 OF AN INCH FROM THE FULL LOCK POSITION.

THE TRIGGER PULL REQUIRED TO RELEASE THE HAMMER SHALL BE SMOOTH, FREE FROM "CREEP," AND WITHIN THE LIMITS OF FOUR AND ONE-HALF TO SIX LBS.

FUNCTIONAL SURFACES OF THE HOOKS OF THE HAMMER AND TRIGGER, AND THE RELATED MATING SURFACES OF THE SEAR MAY HAVE THE PHOSPHATE COATING REMOVED BY POLISHING TO ASSURE SMOOTH TRIGGER PULL.

ESSENTIAL POINTS AND AREAS

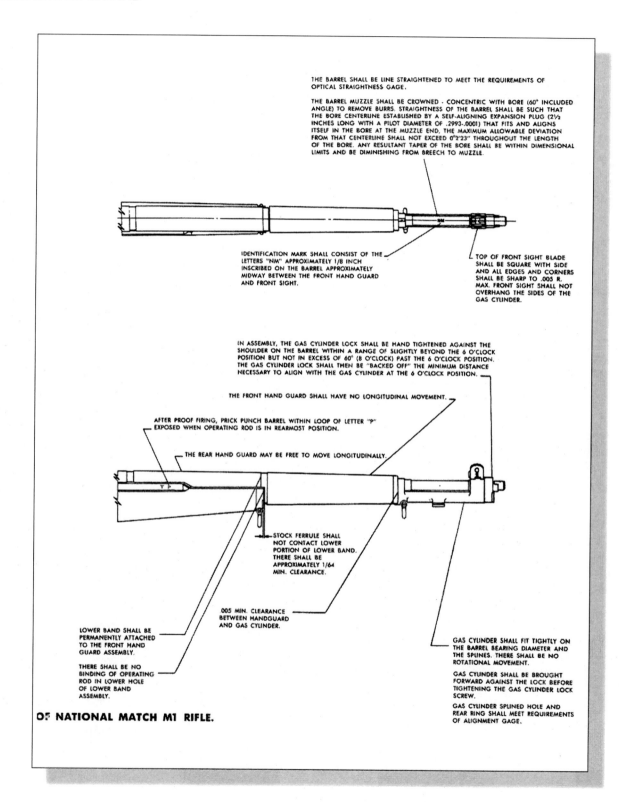

THE BARREL SHALL BE LINE STRAIGHTENED TO MEET THE REQUIREMENTS OF OPTICAL STRAIGHTNESS GAGE.

THE BARREL MUZZLE SHALL BE CROWNED - CONCENTRIC WITH BORE (60° INCLUDED ANGLE) TO REMOVE BURRS. STRAIGHTNESS OF THE BARREL SHALL BE SUCH THAT THE BORE CENTERLINE ESTABLISHED BY A SELF-ALIGNING EXPANSION PLUG (2½ INCHES LONG WITH A PILOT DIAMETER OF .2993-.0001) THAT FITS AND ALIGNS ITSELF IN THE BORE AT THE MUZZLE END, THE MAXIMUM ALLOWABLE DEVIATION FROM THAT CENTERLINE SHALL NOT EXCEED 0°2'23" THROUGHOUT THE LENGTH OF THE BORE. ANY RESULTANT TAPER OF THE BORE SHALL BE WITHIN DIMENSIONAL LIMITS AND BE DIMINISHING FROM BREECH TO MUZZLE.

IDENTIFICATION MARK SHALL CONSIST OF THE LETTERS "NM" APPROXIMATELY 1/8 INCH INSCRIBED ON THE BARREL APPROXIMATELY MIDWAY BETWEEN THE FRONT HAND GUARD AND FRONT SIGHT.

TOP OF FRONT SIGHT BLADE SHALL BE SQUARE WITH SIDE AND ALL EDGES AND CORNERS SHALL BE SHARP TO .005 R. MAX. FRONT SIGHT SHALL NOT OVERHANG THE SIDES OF THE GAS CYLINDER.

IN ASSEMBLY, THE GAS CYLINDER LOCK SHALL BE HAND TIGHTENED AGAINST THE SHOULDER ON THE BARREL WITHIN A RANGE OF SLIGHTLY BEYOND THE 6 O'CLOCK POSITION BUT NOT IN EXCESS OF 60° (8 O'CLOCK) PAST THE 6 O'CLOCK POSITION. THE GAS CYLINDER LOCK SHALL THEN BE "BACKED OFF" THE MINIMUM DISTANCE NECESSARY TO ALIGN WITH THE GAS CYLINDER AT THE 6 O'CLOCK POSITION.

THE FRONT HAND GUARD SHALL HAVE NO LONGITUDINAL MOVEMENT.

AFTER PROOF FIRING, PRICK PUNCH BARREL WITHIN LOOP OF LETTER "P" EXPOSED WHEN OPERATING ROD IS IN REARMOST POSITION.

THE REAR HAND GUARD MAY BE FREE TO MOVE LONGITUDINALLY.

STOCK FERRULE SHALL NOT CONTACT LOWER PORTION OF LOWER BAND. THERE SHALL BE APPROXIMATELY 1/64 MIN. CLEARANCE.

.005 MIN. CLEARANCE BETWEEN HANDGUARD AND GAS CYLINDER.

LOWER BAND SHALL BE PERMANENTLY ATTACHED TO THE FRONT HAND GUARD ASSEMBLY.

THERE SHALL BE NO BINDING OF OPERATING ROD IN LOWER HOLE OF LOWER BAND ASSEMBLY.

GAS CYLINDER SHALL FIT TIGHTLY ON THE BARREL BEARING DIAMETER AND THE SPLINES. THERE SHALL BE NO ROTATIONAL MOVEMENT.

GAS CYLINDER SHALL BE BROUGHT FORWARD AGAINST THE LOCK BEFORE TIGHTENING THE GAS CYLINDER LOCK SCREW.

GAS CYLINDER SPLINED HOLE AND REAR RING SHALL MEET REQUIREMENTS OF ALIGNMENT GAGE.

OF NATIONAL MATCH M1 RIFLE.

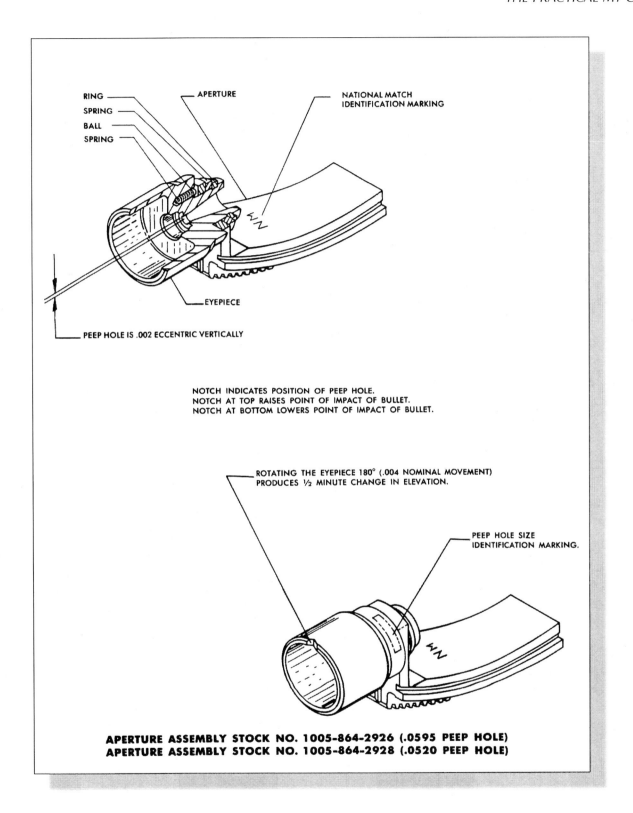

RING
SPRING
BALL
SPRING

APERTURE

NATIONAL MATCH
IDENTIFICATION MARKING

EYEPIECE

PEEP HOLE IS .002 ECCENTRIC VERTICALLY

NOTCH INDICATES POSITION OF PEEP HOLE.
NOTCH AT TOP RAISES POINT OF IMPACT OF BULLET.
NOTCH AT BOTTOM LOWERS POINT OF IMPACT OF BULLET.

ROTATING THE EYEPIECE 180° (.004 NOMINAL MOVEMENT)
PRODUCES ½ MINUTE CHANGE IN ELEVATION.

PEEP HOLE SIZE
IDENTIFICATION MARKING.

APERTURE ASSEMBLY STOCK NO. 1005-864-2926 (.0595 PEEP HOLE)
APERTURE ASSEMBLY STOCK NO. 1005-864-2928 (.0520 PEEP HOLE)

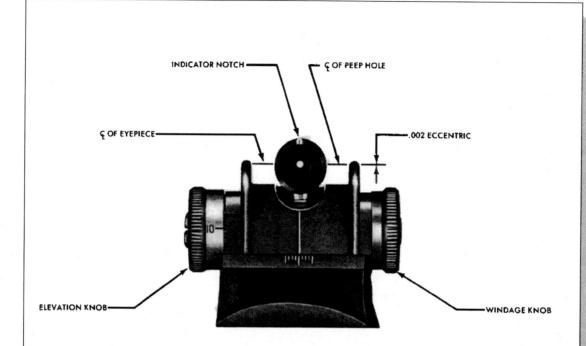

INDICATOR NOTCH ──────── ₵ OF PEEP HOLE

₵ OF EYEPIECE ─────────

.002 ECCENTRIC

ELEVATION KNOB ──────── WINDAGE KNOB

REAR SIGHT MECHANISM FOR ½ MINUTE WINDAGE AND ½ MINUTE ELEVATION

2. SIGHTS

a. The two aperture assemblies are identical except for the eyepieces which have different peep hole diameters. The aperture with .0595 peep hole will be installed as standard with the .0520 diameter aperture available as an alternate.

The hooded eyepiece is designed to eliminate glare and reflections on the sight aperture, and to provide ½ minute changes in elevation.

Each eyepiece is selectively fitted and matched with its individual aperture. It should not be attempted to disassemble the aperture assembly or to change eyepieces on an aperture.

The peep hole is .002 vertically eccentric with other diameters of the eyepiece. Rotating the eyepiece 180° clockwise or counter-clockwise raises and lowers the line of sight. Two spring loaded balls in the eyepiece engage a vertical "v" notch in the face of the aperture to retain the eyepiece in each position. The

position of the eyepiece is indicated by a notch at the rear face of the eyepiece.

Each click of the elevation knob gives a change of 1 minute. Rotating the eyepiece so that the indicator notch is at the top, moves the point of impact of the bullet up ½ minute. With the indicator notch at the bottom, point of impact of the bullet will be moved down ½ minute.

b. The National Match sight base marked NM/2A is undercut to accept the hooded eyepiece. The change from 32 to 64 threads per inch of this sight base and of the windage knob produce a ½ minute change in windage for each click of the knob. Thus the 1963 National Match rifle is capable of ½ minute sight changes for both windage and elevation.

c. The National Match front sight has a blade width of .065 minus .005, and is identified by the letters "NM" and the numbers "062" on its right side. The width of the sight blade of the standard M1 rifle is .084 minus .010.

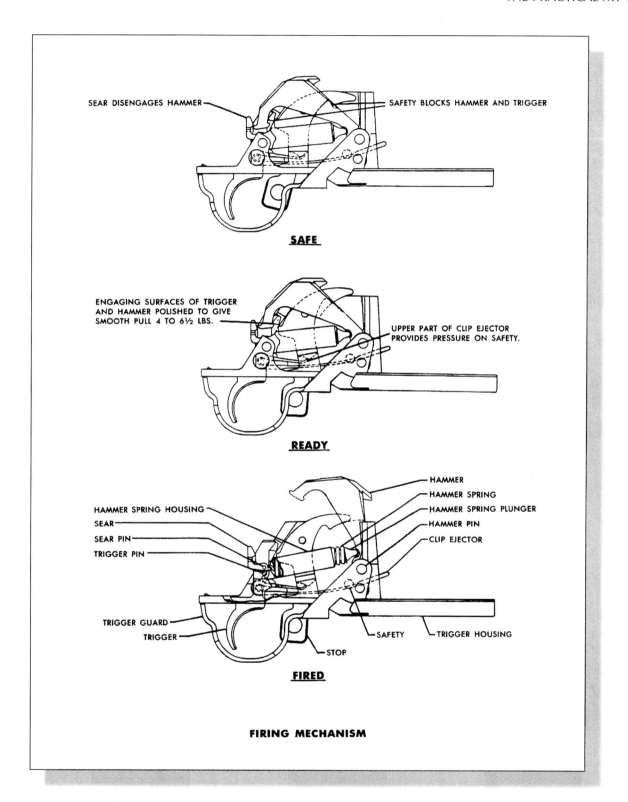

SEAR DISENGAGES HAMMER — SAFETY BLOCKS HAMMER AND TRIGGER

SAFE

ENGAGING SURFACES OF TRIGGER AND HAMMER POLISHED TO GIVE SMOOTH PULL 4 TO 6½ LBS. — UPPER PART OF CLIP EJECTOR PROVIDES PRESSURE ON SAFETY.

READY

HAMMER
HAMMER SPRING
HAMMER SPRING HOUSING
SEAR
HAMMER SPRING PLUNGER
SEAR PIN
HAMMER PIN
TRIGGER PIN
CLIP EJECTOR

TRIGGER GUARD
TRIGGER
SAFETY — TRIGGER HOUSING
STOP

FIRED

FIRING MECHANISM

3. FIRING MECHANISM

The firing mechanism of the National Match M1 rifle is composed of standard parts specially fitted to meet National Match requirements.

The major components of this group are the trigger housing, trigger guard, trigger assembly, safety, hammer, and hammer spring. This group effectively controls the firing of the rifle. To prevent accidental firing, the hammer can be locked in cocked position by the safety. In the event of a misfire, the trigger guard may be used to cock the mechanism.

The rearward movement of the operating rod causes the bolt to move to the rear. The bolt cams the hammer down and rearward and compresses the hammer spring. If at this time the trigger has not been released, the sear engages the rear hammer hooks. Subsequent release of the trigger disengages the sear and allows the hammer to slide into engagement with the trigger lugs. Because of this, a separate squeeze on the trigger is necessary to fire each round.

When the safety is in the rearward (SAFE) position it blocks both the hammer and the trigger.

When the safety is in the forward (READY) position the hammer pivots forward to be engaged, at its front hooks, by the trigger. The hammer and trigger are free to move. Squeezing the trigger disengages the front hooks, and the hammer is driven forward under spring pressure to strike the firing pin and discharge the rifle.

The forward clamping shelf of the trigger housing covers the bottom of the receiver and prevents foreign matter from entering the weapon. The center upright section provides the hole for the hammer pin which serves as a pivot for the hammer and trigger guard. This section also serves as a vertical stop surface for the base of the cartridge clip. The clip ejector positioned at the lower left side of the housing extends through the upright section and exerts continual upward pressure on the clip. Another function of the clip ejector is to spring-load the safety in the selected position. A hole through the upper left side of the housing accommodates the boss of the safety. The trigger pin which passes through the rear section serves as a pivot for the trigger assembly and holds the rear end of the hammer spring housing. The trigger guard is locked in the closed position at the lower rear edge of the housing.

4. GAS CYLINDER

The gas cylinder is a special part and is identified by the letters "NM" on the flat at the rear of the stacking swivel. This gas cylinder is inspected to assure that it fits tightly at the barrel bearing diameter, and that there is no rotational movement of the gas cylinder on the barrel.

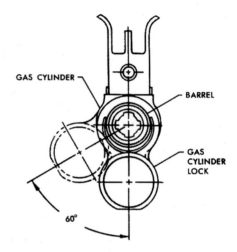

GAS CYLINDER

BARREL

GAS CYLINDER LOCK

60°

FIT OF GAS CYLINDER AND LOCK

The gas cylinder lock should tighten against the shoulder on the barrel within a range of slightly beyond the 6 o'clock position but not in excess of 60° (8 o'clock) beyond the 6 o'clock position. The gas cylinder lock is then "backed off" the minimum distance necessary to align the gas cylinder at the 6 o'clock position.

It is imperative that the gas cylinder lock screw be kept properly tightened.

5. HAND GUARDS

The front hand guard is permanently attached to the lower band. The lower band is pinned to the barrel which eliminates movement of the front hand guard assembly. The stock ferrule at the forward end of the front hand guard must not touch the rear of the gas cylinder.

The rear hand guard may be free to move longitudinally.

PART V — MAINTENANCE

1. CLEANING

When non-corrosive ammunition is used it is not imperative that the bore be cleaned after each day's shooting. If fouling accumulates it may be removed with bore cleaner or solvent. In damp weather a light coat of preservative oil should be left in the bore. Before firing the following day the oil should be removed with dry patches or solvent, and the bore checked for the presence of foreign matter or obstructions. The chamber should be kept clean by using a patch wet with solvent or cleaner on the brush of the chamber cleaning tool. Exterior metal surfaces should be kept clean, and protected with a light coat of preservative oil.

Limited cleaning to prevent fouling build-up in the gas port hole and on the head of the piston may be accomplished without disassembling the rifle. By holding the muzzle down and retracting the operating rod, a small amount of bore cleaner may be poured down the cylindrical portion of the rod and be worked into the gas cylinder. Cleaning without disassembling the rifle aids in maintaining its zero.

APERTURE REAR SIGHT MECHANISM FOR ½ MINUTE WINDAGE AND ELEVATION

2. REAR SIGHT

Sight bases marked NM/2A will accept hooded apertures with .0520 or .0595 peep holes, and also standard (unhooded) apertures. A plastic cap will be provided to protect the aperture assembly.

Changing apertures requires disassembling the rear sight mechanism. Extreme care should be used in handling the parts. Both the windage knob and rear sight base have a fine pitch thread. Because of the precision made threads, particular attention should be given the following, prior to, and during assembly:

a. Insert rear sight base through the opening of the cover.

b. Place the front lip of cover into the recess at the forward portion of rear sight receiver well. Raise the base slightly, exposing the rear portion of the cover. With a screwdriver, apply pressure to rear of cover in a horizontal direction until the cover snaps into place and is firmly retained by the receiver.

c. Insert the aperture, or aperture assembly, into the aperture groove in the base and lower until it bottoms against the receiver.

d. Caution should be exercised in starting windage knob threads into rear sight base to preclude danger of cross threading. Mating threads must be free of excess oil and all foreign matter.

With the left hand, apply pressure to the base forward and to the right of the receiver. Insert and turn windage knob carefully to engage the mating threads. Continue to turn windage knob until the base is tightly seated against the right receiver ear.

e. Insert pinion of elevating knob assembly through the hole on left side of receiver ear, meshing the pinion teeth with mating teeth of the aperture. Simultaneously align by feel, the flat at the end of pinion shaft with mating contour of the lock, housed in the windage knob. Thread the rear sight nut (in the windage knob) onto the pinion shaft. (Some manipulation of parts may be necessary to permit assembly). Tighten rear sight nut until both elevating and windage knobs become inoperative. By backing off the rear sight nut one or more clicks (one-half turn per click) both knobs will then be operative. The graduation mark on rear sight base can be aligned with graduation mark on the receiver.

f. Tighten the rear sight screw securely. Settings of various ranges are attained in terms of the number of clicks from the lowest position of the aperture once the sight has been "zeroed" in at the respective ranges. Once sight settings have been established, the rear sight mechanism should be left intact to preserve sight zero.

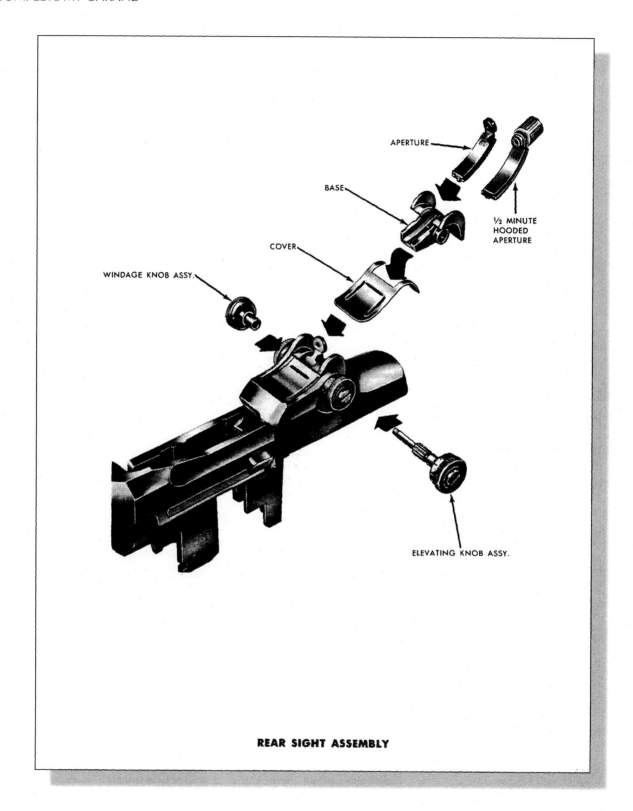

APERTURE

BASE

½ MINUTE
HOODED
APERTURE

COVER

WINDAGE KNOB ASSY.

ELEVATING KNOB ASSY.

REAR SIGHT ASSEMBLY

3. GLASS BEDDING

It has been established that glass bedding improves both accuracy and maintaining of rifle zero.

Pages 17 thru 20 illustrate the method used for glass bedding M1 National Match rifles at Springfield Armory. Preparatory routing of the stock is illustrated below. Standard stocks may be glass bedded if similarly routed.

Materials required for glass bedding are commercially available employing an epoxy resin, milled fiberglass, polyamide resin and catalysts. Prior to using the above materials, it is imperative that a suitable release compound be applied to completely coat those parts of the metal components which will be in contact with the glass bedding. The mold release compound facilitates the breaking away of metal parts, thus leaving an exact molded impression of the metal components. In addition, a suitable solvent should be used for cleaning excess flash in the soft state prior to hardening and for sundry cleaning of equipment. It has been found that the most suitable method for applying glass compound is by the use of a syringe type polyethelene applicator having an orifice of approximately 7/64 or 1/8 inch diameter, effecting a smooth constant extrusion of material into the routed stock channels.

Whenever commercial products are used it is recommended that suppliers' instructions be followed.

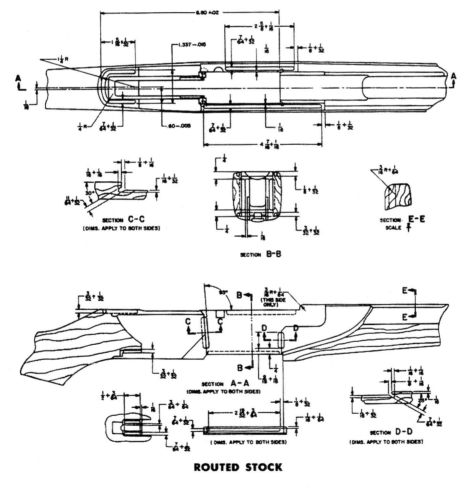

ROUTED STOCK

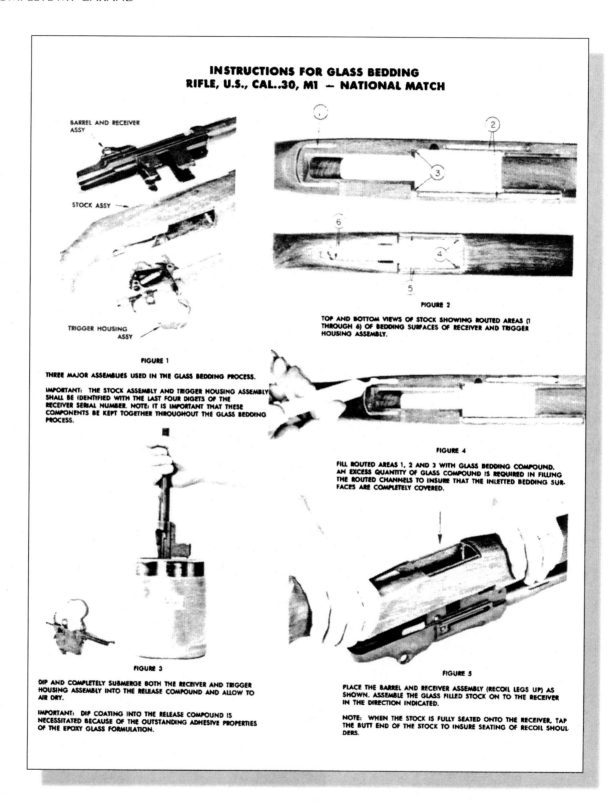

**INSTRUCTIONS FOR GLASS BEDDING
RIFLE, U.S., CAL..30, M1 — NATIONAL MATCH**

BARREL AND RECEIVER ASSY

STOCK ASSY

TRIGGER HOUSING ASSY

FIGURE 1

THREE MAJOR ASSEMBLIES USED IN THE GLASS BEDDING PROCESS.

IMPORTANT: THE STOCK ASSEMBLY AND TRIGGER HOUSING ASSEMBLY SHALL BE IDENTIFIED WITH THE LAST FOUR DIGITS OF THE RECEIVER SERIAL NUMBER. NOTE: IT IS IMPORTANT THAT THESE COMPONENTS BE KEPT TOGETHER THROUGHOUT THE GLASS BEDDING PROCESS.

FIGURE 2

TOP AND BOTTOM VIEWS OF STOCK SHOWING ROUTED AREAS (1 THROUGH 6) OF BEDDING SURFACES OF RECEIVER AND TRIGGER HOUSING ASSEMBLY.

FIGURE 4

FILL ROUTED AREAS 1, 2 AND 3 WITH GLASS BEDDING COMPOUND. AN EXCESS QUANTITY OF GLASS COMPOUND IS REQUIRED IN FILLING THE ROUTED CHANNELS TO INSURE THAT THE INLETTED BEDDING SURFACES ARE COMPLETELY COVERED.

FIGURE 3

DIP AND COMPLETELY SUBMERGE BOTH THE RECEIVER AND TRIGGER HOUSING ASSEMBLY INTO THE RELEASE COMPOUND AND ALLOW TO AIR DRY.

IMPORTANT: DIP COATING INTO THE RELEASE COMPOUND IS NECESSITATED BECAUSE OF THE OUTSTANDING ADHESIVE PROPERTIES OF THE EPOXY GLASS FORMULATION.

FIGURE 5

PLACE THE BARREL AND RECEIVER ASSEMBLY (RECOIL LEGS UP) AS SHOWN. ASSEMBLE THE GLASS FILLED STOCK ON TO THE RECEIVER IN THE DIRECTION INDICATED.

NOTE: WHEN THE STOCK IS FULLY SEATED ONTO THE RECEIVER, TAP THE BUTT END OF THE STOCK TO INSURE SEATING OF RECOIL SHOULDERS.

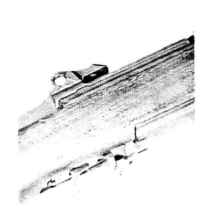

FIGURE 6

1. CLAMP THE TRIGGER GUARD TO WITHIN 1/4 INCH OF THE FULL LOCK POSITION. THE TRIGGER GUARD CAN BE HELD IN THIS POSITION WITH THE USE OF A U-SHAPED RETAINER AND/OR PIN.

NOTE: CAUTION SHALL BE EXERCISED TO INSURE THAT TRIGGER GUARD DOES NOT EXCEED ITS 1/4 INCH OPENING. SAFETY SHOULD BE IN "SAFE" POSITION.

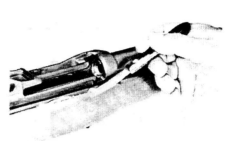

FIGURE 7

REMOVE EXCESS GLASS COMPOUND DISPLACED AFTER ACTION IS CLAMPED. FINAL TRACES OF GLASS COMPOUND SHOULD BE WIPED CLEAN.

THE COMPLETE ACTION SHALL BE ALLOWED TO DRY A MINIMUM OF 8 HOURS.

FIGURE 8

DISASSEMBLE THE BARREL AND RECEIVER ASSEMBLY FROM THE STOCK ASSEMBLY AS FOLLOWS:

1. REMOVE THE TRIGGER HOUSING ASSEMBLY.

2. HOLDING THE ASSEMBLY AS SHOWN IN FIGURE 8, STRIKE A SOLID SURFACE WITH THE BUTT END OF THE STOCK TO DISLODGE THE RECEIVER IN THE DIRECTION SHOWN.

3. EXAMINE STOCK TO INSURE THAT A DEFINITE IMPRESSION OF THE RECEIVER BEARING SURFACES HAS BEEN MADE OF THE GLASS BEDDED AREAS OF THE STOCK.

4. CLEAN ALL EXCESSES OF GLASS COMPOUND FROM METAL (RECEIVER & TRIGGER HOUSING ASSY) AND FROM ADJACENT AREAS OF BEDDED SURFACES OF STOCK.

5. IMPORTANT: MAKE SURE THAT THE MOLDED IMPRESSION OF THE RECEIVER BEARING SURFACES ARE NOT DISTURBED WHEN THE SOLIDIFIED EXCESSES OF GLASS COMPOUND ARE REMOVED.

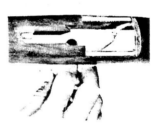

FIGURE 9

1. REDIP AND COMPLETELY SUBMERGE BOTH THE BARREL AND RECEIVER ASSY AND TRIGGER HOUSING ASSY.

2. FILL ROUTED AREAS 4, 5 AND 6 WITH AN EXCESS OF GLASS BEDDING COMPOUND.

FIGURE 10

1. PLACE THE BARREL AND RECEIVER ASSEMBLY (RECOIL LEGS UP) AS SHOWN. ASSEMBLE THE GLASS FILLED STOCK (AREAS 4, 5 & 6) ON TO THE RECEIVER IN DIRECTION INDICATED.

2. CLAMP THE TRIGGER HOUSING ASSEMBLY AND POSITION THE TRIGGER GUARD WITH THE "U" SHAPED LOCK AS SHOWN IN FIGURE 11.

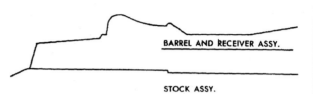

BARREL AND RECEIVER ASSY.

STOCK ASSY.

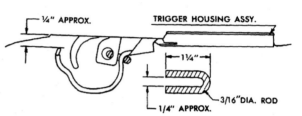

¼" APPROX.

TRIGGER HOUSING ASSY.

1¼"

3/16"DIA. ROD

¼" APPROX.

FIGURE 11

CONFIGURATION AND USE OF U LOCK.

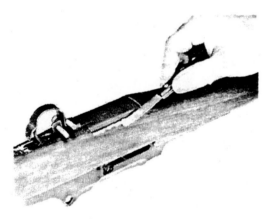

FIGURE 12

1. REMOVE EXCESS GLASS COMPOUND FROM ACTION AS DESCRIBED IN FIGURE 7.

2. ALLOW THE ACTION TO DRY A MINIMUM PERIOD OF 8 HOURS.

3. DISASSEMBLE THE BARREL AND RECEIVER ASSEMBLY FROM THE STOCK ASSEMBLY AS DESCRIBED UNDER FIGURE 8.

4. EXAMINE STOCK TO INSURE THAT A DEFINITE IMPRESSION OF RECEIVER AND TRIGGER HOUSING BEARING SURFACES HAS BEEN MADE ON GLASS BEDDED AREAS OF THE STOCK.

5. IMPORTANT: INSURE THAT THE MOLDED IMPRESSION OF THE RECEIVER AND TRIGGER HOUSING SURFACES ARE NOT DISTURBED WHEN THE SOLIDIFIED EXCESSES OF GLASS COMPOUND ARE REMOVED.

FIGURE 13

TOP AND BOTTOM VIEWS OF COMPLETED GLASS BEDDED STOCK.

III

THE GARAND, ILLUSTRATED AND EXPLAINED

The M1 was produced more or less continuously in the United States for 20 years and in Italy until at least the late 1960s. That's a gross military production life of about 32 years. Add on another 20 years of civilian production.

The photos and subsections in Part III describe the rifles and are intended to help the collector or shooter identify and categorize his rifle and its parts.

Later in this book are some further details in a special "parts" area, which will demonstrate how every single part of the Garand—even though most will interchange from the very first to the very last rifle—became a whole different item.

The background presented in the preceding history of the rifle should help put these photos in context easily.

WARTIME GARANDS

Early and World War II Garands, photos 28-54 (pp. 78-86): Prewar and World War II Garands are the most active areas for collectors, the least active for shooters.

The gas trap gun with its 22-inch barrel and internal blast cone configuration, was a loser from the first day, just as similar designs failed in Germany, England, Belgium, and Russia. Nobody ever got the elegant theory to work properly in the field, mainly because of the tremendous mass of hot gas that had to be moved around. By serial #55,844, the gas trap rifle was pretty much a dead horse, though a few higher-numbered specimens have supposedly been identified. The experimental "gas port" rifle (a 24-inch-barreled gun with an approximately 5/64-inch gas hole exiting into a much smaller chamber in a new gas cylinder) comprised a considerable number of guns numbered below 50,000, of which numbers 43938 and 44602 are two confirmed specimens. Rifle #44702 (shown on p. 81) may be another early gas port experimental, though it is impossible to prove. Most likely it was built as a gas trap gun but did not stay that way for very long. What you need to know is that you will never find a "gas trap" rifle that is both intact and cheap. And restoring one of the low-numbered guns is a process that is brutally expensive, close to impossible, and ultimately amounts to taking a gun that probably works rather well and making it into a version of same whose function is, at best, questionable. Right now, the approximate dollar figure required to "revert" a low-numbered gun using mostly custom-made reproduction parts is a minimum of roughly $2,000. With authentic parts? Forget it.

There are some other asides that intrigue some collectors, at least one of which is almost impossible to illustrate adequately in a black-and-white book. Suppose you find a Garand with a horrendous looking scorch mark, blackish at the rear, fading to dark grays and even browns at the front. A much-feared "REMIL"? A gun that's been in a fire? Sort of the latter. A new grenade launcher introduced in 1943 tended to crack some of the harder (as in more brittle) receivers, and so a new heat-treat configuration was applied to some existing receivers and a few that had not yet left the factory. This process is the source of the "two-tones." If the "scorch" mark is especially profound, the gun still bears its original finish and is therefore worth a little bit extra because of its unique and obvious background. Suppose you notice a "hot spot" of weld about 3/4 inch back on the op rod channel (groove) front border on the raceway flat on the receiver's right. Is this a reweld? Sort of. If the serial number is below 80,000 or so, the hot spot marks some of the work required to prevent the much-vaunted "seventh round stoppage." (Some rifles up to 96,000 were so treated; virtually all below 80,000 were.)

Some other notes: virtually all Winchester receivers, up until the WIN-13 series, were of the very early -2 version, which had square cutout rear of bolt travel on the receiver (see Photos 65-67)—a feature that was gone from Springfield production by 1941. Winchesters are rough receivers, and many of their trigger parts are even rougher. While they are a poor choice for shooters because of the weaker earlier receiver design and the usual out-of-specification condition of many—if not most—of the parts, they can shoot fairly well with excellent barrels. These Winchesters are worth entirely too much money to devote much more to converting a receiver to anything like match configuration.

By 1945 the Armory was well into -35 receivers, which were much stronger than the units of 1941. The most common receiver variants are shown here along with some rare specimens, such as the very first Winchester rifle produced. Winchester never built a gas trap rifle.

The observer will note that many of my rifles of World War II vintage in these pages bear the much later National Match rear sight aperture. This takes a few seconds to install and is a much better sight than the military version; I use it on any M1 I shoot. I generally change out only sights and operating rods when I shoot vintage Garands.

Certain standard equipment had to be replaced at war's end with almost indecent haste. Replacing or modifying uncut operating rods was a safety priority, but it is amazing how many show up on MAP returnees and even DCM guns. Both early sight styles were basically failures, and the third type was added to virtually all World War II guns during rebuilds. The section on rebuilds (p. 94-97) and various other photos in this book document these alterations.

Just as parts and receivers changed, so did markings. Early barrels did not carry dates. Standard Winchester barrels never carried dates, though I have seen what may be replacements or fakes that did. Ironically, these were cases where the low prices suggested to me that the barrels might have been authentic, *though I very much doubt they were issue barrels of any sort.* I suspect they were part of some kind of subcontracting deal that either fell through or comprised a very small lot of replacement units or experimentals.

Even into the postwar era, replacement barrels as late as 1951 used the World War II marking pattern, with the maker information atop the barrel. By 1953 (earlier at Springfield Armory) subcontractors placed maker and date information neatly in the operating rod cutout, between the buttstock and the rear handguard.

Everything on the Garand got continuously better as production wore on. By 1943 the early, intricate milled trigger guard was replaced with a spring steel stamping, which proved easier to adjust and more durable. By mid-1942 the gas cylinder's bulk and strength were increased. The "X-form" gas cylinder lock screw allowed the use of a new grenade launcher and introduced an additional safety factor.

Checking the parts details section later in this book will give the reader some idea as to how various complex parts were replaced with stronger, simpler items as time wore on. This may be the central lesson of the Garand's evolution: Simpler is better.

• • • • •

Springfield

Gas trap rifles, photos 28-34 (pp. 78-79) and illustration (p. 80): Virtually all M1 Garands numbered below 50,000 were originally gas trap rifles, as were a few experimentals above that figure. However, virtually all have been reconfigured during their long lives to the ubiquitous "gas port" configuration. The rare rifle shown in the detail photos here is serial #26171 and remains in its original ca. 1939 configuration. Comparison of this rifle with other gas traps reflects the tremendous amount of fine-tuning done virtually continuously (though somewhat erratically) on all the early Garands.

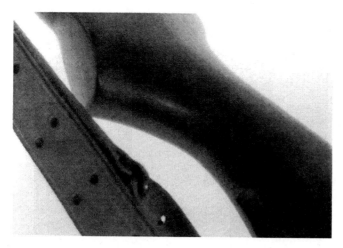

PHOTO 28. Many of the early rifles never received cartouches.

PHOTO 29. Virtually every part of the "gas trap" rifle was different from the "typical" gas port rifle—even the "square" (flattened) configuration of the recoil spring. The entire operating mechanism—operating rod catch, follower rod and arm, bullet guide—is shaped very differently from later guns. Note also the creased surface of the handguard clip.

PHOTO 30. The gas trap gas cylinder was much more massive and entirely different from all others. The barrel ended less than halfway down the upper "tube," and the gas cylinder was screwed on. This was secured by two screws. The "muzzle" was a false muzzle, in fact part of the gas cylinder. The sight and its attachment are entirely different from the gas port style. There were several other subtypes of this gas cylinder, all shaped more or less the same, but with tool grip flutes added to some.

PHOTO 31. The original buttplate contained no accessory or oiler door at all.

PHOTO 32. The heavy creased and scalloped bands of the gas trap guns were carried over to early gas port rifles.

PHOTO 33. The early "First Model" sight and cover and early receiver configuration of rifle #26171.

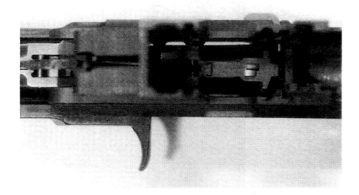

PHOTO 34. Follower well and bullet guide view, from bottom, of serial #26171.

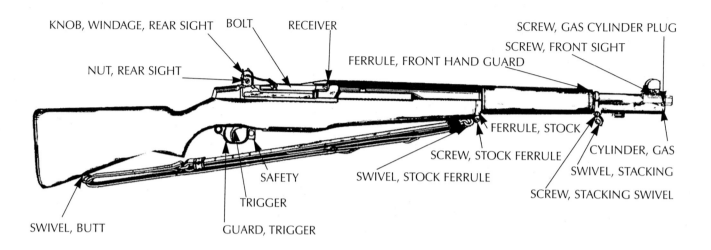

KNOB, WINDAGE, REAR SIGHT   BOLT   RECEIVER   SCREW, GAS CYLINDER PLUG

SCREW, FRONT SIGHT

NUT, REAR SIGHT   FERRULE, FRONT HAND GUARD

KNOB, WINDAGE, REAR SIGHT

FERRULE, STOCK

SCREW, STOCK FERRULE   CYLINDER, GAS

SAFETY   SWIVEL, STOCK FERRULE   SWIVEL, STACKING

TRIGGER   SCREW, STACKING SWIVEL

SWIVEL, BUTT   GUARD, TRIGGER

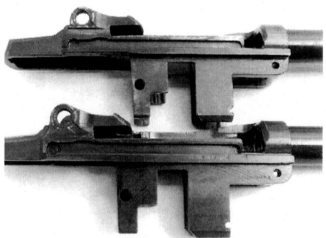

PHOTO 35. Garand receivers from the rifle's early production, from top, 97308, 7146, and 44555. Note squared-off rear receiver legs on all. Note also the traces of welding on 7146 and 44555, done during their changeover from "gas trap" configuration to obviate the "seventh-round stoppage."

PHOTO 36. A direct comparison of -2 receivers from Springfield Armory and Winchester (the Springfield D2821-2 on the top and the Winchester on the bottom), both delivered by late 1941. Winchester's overall quality and conformance to specifications, even simple dimensional specifications, was very questionable, which can be proven very quickly with a micrometer. The poor machining on the Winchester is quite visible on the strut/lug area adjacent to the part numbers. Winchester continued to produce this comparatively primitive receiver type right up until the WIN-13 series, by which time the armory had produced at least 35 major improvements.

Note that both receivers, at this stage, retained the square bolt cutout and that the leading edges of the rear stock engagement lug ("strut") still had not received the softened edges standardized by 1942.

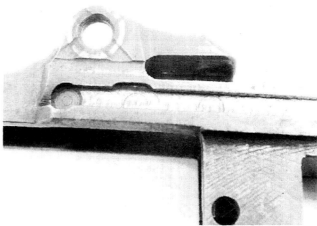

PHOTO 37. Rifle serial #44702 may have been an experimental "gas port" rifle (verifiably, #44602 was such an experiment), but it is more likely the gun was simply reconfigured to the later model very early in its service life. Note that, rebuilt or not, the rifle retained all its early parts, even the flush nut sights.

PHOTO 38. By the -3 revision, the Garand receiver was already becoming more streamlined and sturdy. This modification, with the rounded bolt cutout, seems to have been produced for a time alongside the earlier -2 type.

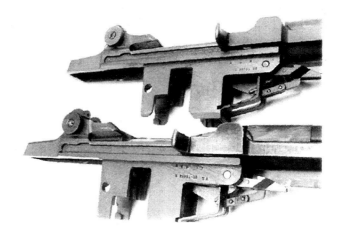

PHOTO 39. Extremely rare, totally unblemished cartouching on an early 1941 issue lend-lease Garand. This unfired gun, returned from England in the late 1940s, has apparently never seen any of the sanding to which most stateside rifles were repeatedly subjected. The barrel bears full British proofs of the period. The SA/GHS cartouched stock, by itself, could be sold for more than the DCM acquisition price of an M1 Garand. This one, though, is likely a Galef "reimport" from 50 years ago.

PHOTO 40. A comparison between a ca. 1941 receiver (-13, bottom) and a rebuilt ca. 1945 receiver (-35, top) reveals that machine tool quality and precision improved even as Garand production pace increased. Note the virtual absence of tool marks on the later specimen, as opposed to the severe drag marks on the earlier rifle. The later receiver is also considerably stronger in key areas.

PHOTO 41. The rounded bolt cutout generic to the -3 receivers and some other improvements were incorporated earlier than sometimes believed, or perhaps unfinished -2 units were simply completed with the -3 improvements. This one is marked D 28291-2 but bears all the -3 modifications.

PHOTO 42. This -3 receiver overlaps the period of time within which only -2s were supposedly leaving the armory. But its other parts (cartouche, etc.) suggest an actual delivery date just when the receiver configuration would suggest.

PHOTO 43. This -14 receiver shows fairly typical early midwar characteristics. Note the rounded receiver struts.

PHOTO 44. By the -17 revision, ca. 1942, the Garand had reached its "definitive" World War II receiver configuration. The striations on this one are very rare by this vintage and are probably caused by a nearly worn-out tool. Note the various witness marks and codes above the part number.

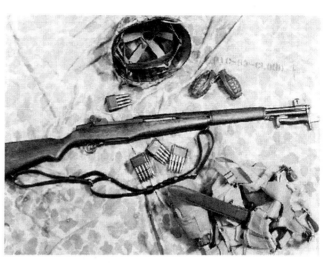

PHOTO 45. Typical Springfield barrel markings, these from August 1943.

PHOTO 46. Typical midwar Springfield M1 Garand, ca. 1943, with bayonet affixed, surrounded by vintage USMC memorabilia. The rifle probably saw service at Iwo Jima.

PHOTO 47. When World War II Garands had been sighted and test-fired and were ready to leave the armory, a seal was driven into the Allen screw at the rear of each rifle's front sight. Very few rifles retain these seals.

PHOTO 48. Comparison photo of three M1 Garands: (top) 1940—note especially the "first model" flush nut rear sight; (middle) 1941; (bottom) mid-1942.

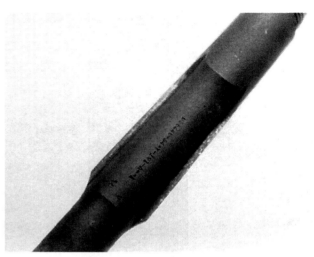

PHOTO 49. Typical stock cartouches on as-issued rifles received from Arlington Ordnance. Both have been rebuilt once, and the top rifle has had its stamped trigger guard replaced with an older milled unit during the process. Both rifles date from 1945, though the lower rifle may not have been actually completed until after the war, and its 2-46 dated barrel may, therefore, be its original. The top cartouche is SA/NFR (Norman F. Ramsey), the lower, the rare SHM (Steven H. MacGregor), ca. 1946.

PHOTO 50. Late World War II Springfield barrels carried their part number and detailed information—lot and heat treat numbers—atop the chamber area, under the wood. Early war rifles, of course, carried all the data here, as Winchesters always did.

Winchester

Winchester's first M1 Garand, photos 51-56 (pp. 85-86): Laying hands on Winchester's very first M1 Garand was an exciting experience, and studying the rifle was an education—just as this rifle itself was an educational tool for workers at Winchester. This first batch of rifles essentially consisted of handmade early "gas port" rifles of the -2 version then being made at Springfield. The gun seems to be satin blued or phosphated, then hydroxide dipped to produce a semigloss black finish that resembles a nicely applied coat of black trim paint.

In order to photograph Larry Kaufman's rare rifle and get some contrast on the markings where necessary, I used a technique others might find convenient: a quick, temporary surface burnish applied simply by rubbing the area with aluminum foil. This allows the original stampings to show well without having to apply anything permanent and without impossible lighting problems that make the surface look artificial. This burnish may then be wiped off with thin oil, rifle bore cleaner, or any convenient petroleum-based solvent. Note the typical "electric writing" of the Winchester logo.

PHOTO 51.

PHOTOS 52 and 53. Two rare early trigger groups: on the left, from Kaufman's gas trap, with extra hole and unfinished hammer spring plunger, and on the right the "closed" side of the very first Winchester M1. Both evince considerable rough machine work. Much later Winchester production is not much different.

PHOTO 54. The early, narrow-profile gas cylinder of 100001 carries its part number on the rear, upper "hoop."

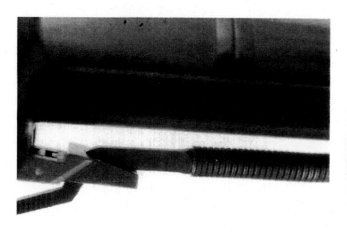

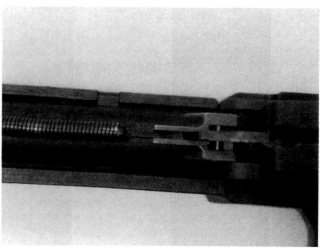

PHOTOS 55 and 56. All of the first Winchester's operating rod assembly parts are typical, heavily marked, milled series similar to early Springfield parts.

Early and midwar Winchester M1 Garands, photos 57-64 (pp. 87-88): The Winchester Garand did not change much after the very first rifle. Virtually all parts remained the same or very similar, though some subcontractor parts (marked "A" or "CM") were used as the pace of production sped up.

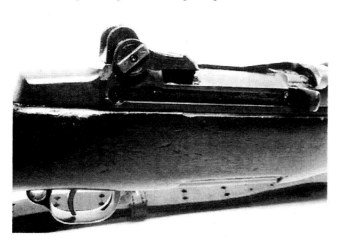

PHOTO 57. Midwar Winchester as rebuilt around 1947.

PHOTO 58. View of receiver of a midwar Winchester Garand from the bottom. Note short fork follower rod and milled, serrated "A" on bullet guide.

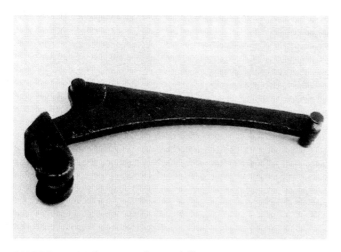

PHOTO 59. Midwar Winchester follower arm.

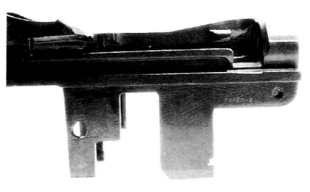

PHOTO 60. Side view, midwar Winchester receiver.

PHOTO 61. Trigger guard part number data stamping on mid-war Winchester M1.

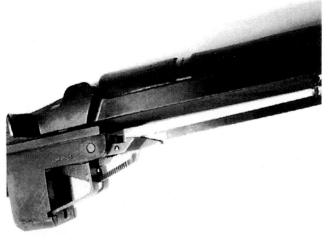

PHOTO 62. Side view (right) of early war M1 Garand, destocked.

PHOTO 63. Midwar Winchester M1 Garand trigger housing.

PHOTO 64. Closeup of witness marks below front right bolt lug detent on receiver of a midwar Winchester M1.

PHOTO 65. Winchester receiver #130081.   PHOTO 66. Winchester receiver #1332557.

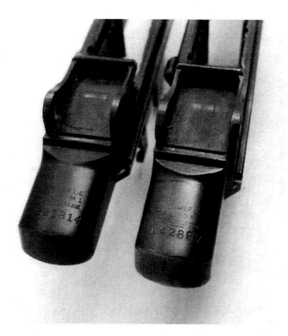 

PHOTO 67. Comparison shot of late Winchester M1 receivers #2321814 (ca. 1945) and #142897 (ca. 1941) demonstrates how little these changed in the time frame in which the armory had instituted 35 major changes.

PHOTO 68. Winchester receiver #2310946. As with most of the Winchester receivers in these photos, this is an Arlington Ordnance "reimport" that has never been refinished.

The WIN-13 Series, photos 69-72 (pp. 91-92): The WIN-13 series constitutes the very last Winchester M1 Garands, in which some of the early parts array and configuration were discarded. These rifles are, at least in theory, the only American-made Garands whose serial numbers are directly duplicated. The close-ups here are of receiver #1617139, which (alone among the Winchesters pictured here) bears a fairly typical "charcoal" phosphate finish.

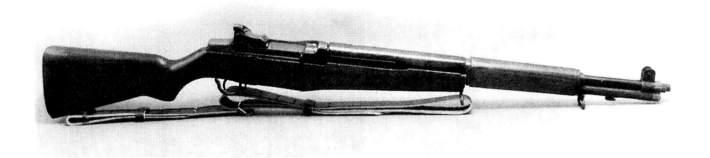

PHOTO 69. WIN-13 rifle with very late finish and -9 configuration operation rod. NOTE: National Match sight aperture was added by the author for firing convenience and is not authentic or original. Stamped trigger guard was on rifle when received and is probably not original, though finish does match receiver's "charcoal" exactly.

PHOTO 70. Close-up of WIN-13 receiver serial #1617139.

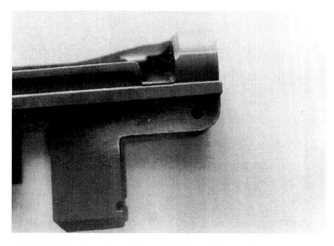

PHOTO 71. Burnished for visibility, this marking panel on #1617139's receiver reads "D28291WIN-13."

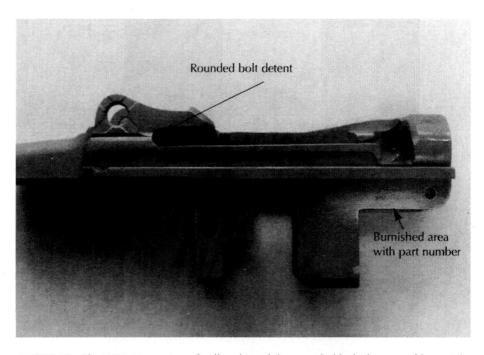

PHOTO 72. The WIN-13 receivers finally adopted the rounded bolt detent and later sight "click" cuts. Note the part number and updated overall contours.

WORLD WAR II SERIAL NUMBERS, AS ALLOCATED

Manufacturer	Blocks, as Assigned
SA	1–100,000
WRA	100,001–165,000
SA	165,001–1,200,000
WRA	1,200,001–1,357,473
SA	1,357,474–2,305,849
WRA	2,305,850–2,655,982
SA	2,655,983–4,100,000

The actual "last" M1 receiver delivered on World War II contracts was in the high 3,900,000 range.

The world abounds with date charts for M1 Garands, and they're generally close. However, the dates are always derived from contract information, and thus the actual delivery or barrel date of a Garand will almost always be later than the "book" date. Wartime and postwar cartouches, likewise, do not necessarily have much do with actual delivery dates. I've handled a WIN-13 Winchester, for example (none of which were delivered until after the war) that bore a WRA/WB stock, and, based on the circumstances of the rifle's acquisition, it almost had to be the "issue" stock for the rifle. Such anomalies are less common on Springfield guns but do exist, since factories tended not to throw away usable material of any kind, and perhaps their last concern during World War II was what some collector would think more than 50 years down the line.

These letter combinations (as the illustrations make clear) appear right where your cheek goes in the firing position—stock's left side, just below the "heel" of the receiver and slightly to the front.

Cartouche	I.D. & service period	Appx. serial # range	Notes
SA/SPG	Samuel P. Green	1–80,000	all gas trap and early gas port rifles
SA/GHS	Col. Gilbert H. Stewart Mid 1940–June 1942	80,000–700,000	early WWII
SA/EMcF	Col. Earl McFarland June 1942–July 1943	700,000–1,800,000	midwar
SA/GAW	Col. George A. Woody July 1943–October 1944	1,800,000–3,260,000	late war
SA/NFR	Gen. Norman F. Ramsey Oct. 1944–Nov. 1945 rifles	3,260,000–3,900,000+	last wartime
SA/SHM	Col. Steven H. MacGregor Nov. 1945–Aug. 1947	—	small production, experimentals, much rebuild activity
SA/JLG	Col. James L. Guion	4,200,000–4,300,000	a very few "Korean War" rifles, by comparison, got letter cartouches before the defense acceptance stamp was standardized

Cartouche	I.D. & service period	Appx. serial # range	Notes
WRA/WB	Col. Waldemar Broberg 1940-1941	100,001–appx. 1,220,000	
WRA/RS	Col. Robert Sears 1941-1942	1,220,000–appx. 1,357,473	
WRA/GHD	Col. Guy H. Drewry*	at least 1,357,473–2,655,982 and WIN-13 series	

* All Winchester cartouche data is to be taken with a grain of salt, as are many so-called "rules" of parts marking. Collectors have seen, owned, and handled enough rifles to know that so-called "early" wood was leaving the factory right up until the very end. Serial #100,001 (pictured in this book) has a certifiably original stock and never had a cartouche.

Rebuilds

Throughout their production career and long after (well into the 1970s) M1 Garands were rebuilt in a bewildering variety of facilities all over the world. A major book could easily be written dealing merely with the types, patterns, and remarkings of various Garand rebuilds. A great deal of the research would have to be based on speculation, though, for the records of bases all over the world would prove virtually impossible to reconstruct.

This small subsection on rebuilds is included separately to give the reader a flavor for what rebuild markings look like.

Certain details of early rebuilds—which began, incidentally, as early as 1940—were urgent. The conversion from "gas trap" to "gas port" operating system was a matter of great priority. Later, so were the removal of both the flush nut and later locking bar sights. Most critical was the replacement or modification of uncut, square-cornered operating rods, which was a matter of safety.

Considering the clarity of the orders of the time, it is amazing that many of the old operating rods survived. In fact, many postwar rifles were rebuilt using World War II and even prewar parts as time wore on. That is the source of the mixed-up parts brand and vintages on so very many rifles. There is one fairly reliable rule of thumb, though: one can be reasonably certain that a wartime part on a postwar rifle did not go through Springfield Armory's rebuild programs, whereas a newer part on an older rifle—especially if the pattern is consistent— strongly indicates that the rebuild was executed either by the armory or by someone who read the Technical Operations Orders governing such refurbishments.

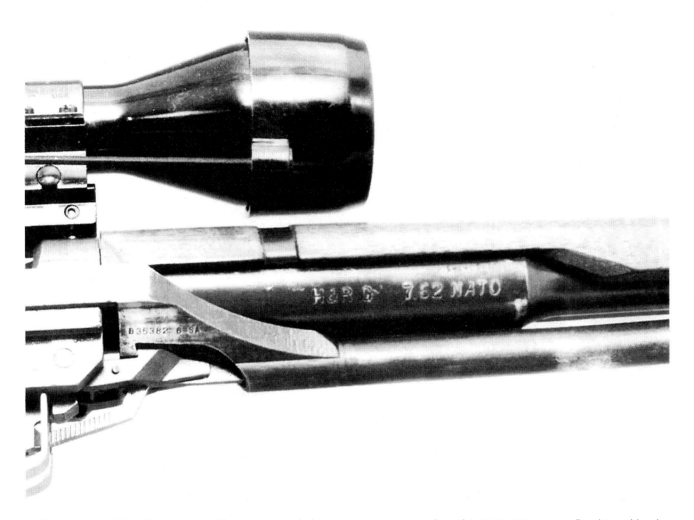

PHOTO 73. Rebuilding World War II rifles sometimes led to some strange anomalies. This 2,900,000 range rifle, shipped by the DCM and shown here wearing a B-Square scope mount and 3-9x glass, was received with a -6 uncut operating rod and this very unusual barrel (of Springfield manufacture, bearing an original 1948 date) but in 7.62 NATO and not bearing a chamber bushing or sleeve of any kind, indicating that at least some of the armory's production must have been set aside with no chamber reamed at all. The rebuild seems to have been done at H&R sometime in the 1960s.

PHOTO 74. A Springfield Armory replacement barrel, produced in May 1951. The postwar part number is D 6535448, located on the barrel's upper surface.

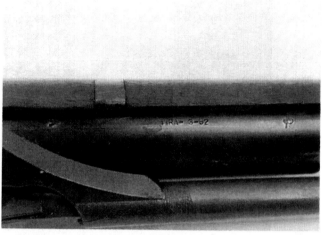

PHOTO 75. Marking on a 3-52 dated H&R replacement barrel. Though barrels marked in this manner are often found on rifles of approximately the same vintage, it is virtually certain that these are, in fact, replacement units from separate contracts, since issue barrels contained the full data panel on the right side, and the "original" barrels at H&R did not enter production until a few months later.

PHOTO 76. Almost immediately at the end of World War II, it was necessary to update and rehabilitate a great many veteran rifles, including this 120,000 unit, rebuilt in early 1946. Most of the original parts survived, though the operating rod was modified, the barrel replaced, and a then-new "SHM" cartouched stock fitted. Replacement of the extant sights with the "type 3" was a priority because of problems with locking and unlocking both previous sight styles.

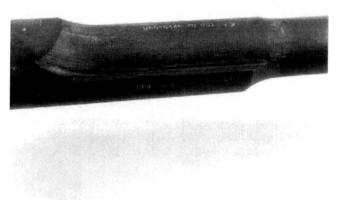

PHOTO 77. View of 3-52 H&R replacement barrel, showing both information panels.

PHOTO 78. Aniston Arsenal often applied lot and order numbers to stock wood on rebuilds. This one is from the early 1950s.

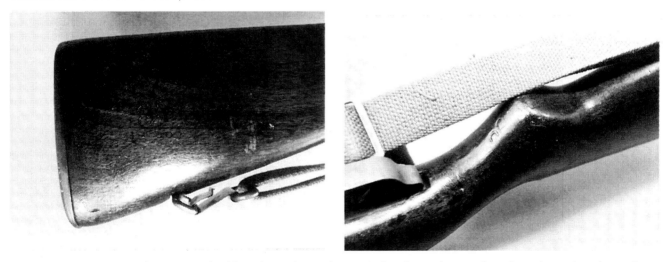

PHOTOS 79, 80. Commonly, postwar rebuilds replicate the "P" firing proof on the stock—usually without the serifs and quite large and deep with no circle around the letter—and often they replicate the last two or three digits of the rifle's serial number on the stock (if the stock required repair).

The following serial number information pertains to wartime lots allocated, which (as the reader will note from the data) does not necessarily indicate that a rifle was built, or built as allocated. For example, most of Winchester's WIN-13 series were numbered, almost spitefully, to overlap Springfield Armory's 1.6 million block.

About 220,000 of Springfield's last wartime serial number block were not manufactured, a great many of them having apparently been assigned to Remington in pursuit of the slightly longer upper-receivered selective-fire T22. Indeed, much later, H&R built a very few 7.62x51mm rifles in Springfield's very last (over 6 million) lot, apparently to serve as ammunition workup guns for the M14, which was about to enter production.

THE POSTWAR GARANDS

The wartime M1 Garand may be the typical, "definitive," and most common M1 Garand, but the postwar rifles are unquestionably the best, and for very simple reasons: they're newer and have therefore been knocked around less; they were made without the pressure of an ongoing "hot" war; and they reflect all the technological and safety improvements of 16 years' research, experience, and progress. The "special purpose" guns wound up seeing much of their use postwar as well, though many were based upon wartime receivers.

In addition to parts sections scattered throughout this book, this short preface to the postwar manufacturers (Springfield Armory [U.S.], H&R, International Harvester, Beretta, and Springfield Armory, Incorporated [private firm]) includes some photos to give the reader some idea of the new assemblies incorporated into the 1950 and later guns.

Almost all postwar parts were improved and renumbered, prefixed "55," "65," and, in the case of the operating rod, "77" on the very last batches.

There were other manufacturers who produced nonspecification cast receivers. Apparently the Breda organization actually built receivers, although Beretta eventually absorbed its production capability. I have never seen a Breda receiver and would not be especially surprised to find out that there were none.

Remington seems to have produced a considerable quantity of experimental T22 selective-fire receivers, which were longer and employed a trigger-based selector setup.

International Harvester rifles are a fascinating corporate and hardware study. Historians continually puzzle over why IHC was ever brought into any firearms procurement program, especially when there were competent, well-established precision firearms firms in the United States who could have used the work. The tractor and truck producer had no firearms background and had constant quality and delivery difficulties; one researcher estimates that roughly 15 to 20 percent of its production actually occurred at Springfield Armory and at least another 10 to 15 percent was finished or detail-inspected by Springfield staff. Two indicators of IHC's difficulties come from even a quick inspection of its receivers, which show odd contour permutations at random and large variations in finish color (often running to strange dark green), which most experts feel indicates poor chemical control or contamination of the phosphate chemicals.

All postwar Garands were issued with the stamped trigger guard, though in the rebuilding process many milled guards got stuck on postwar rifles. Most shooters prefer the stamped unit, made out of spring steel, which is more readily adjusted if it gets out of whack and evinces greater tensile strength.

Unique among Garands, most Beretta rifles carried their serial number and identifier data on the left rearmost receiver flat, just behind and below the elevation knob, on the left. Some very late rifles are marked on the "horseshoe," just like their American counterparts. Beretta's production is covered in far greater detail than here in Vol. 7, No. 2 of the *Garand Collector's Association Newsletter* (pp. 6-12), in an article by Corso P. Boccia.

Covered later on in this book are the spin-offs of the Garand, including the BM.59s, most of which actually began life as M1s and were modified to the later format.

That Beretta, F.N., and Sauer parts are found on M1s—even DCM guns, which saw NATO service—should amaze no one. Rifles were being rebuilt in Europe just as they were in the United States.

The M1 is the "daddy" of the M14, but the adoption of the 7.62mm.x51 cartridge in Europe prompted some changes in the M1 that, until recently, went largely unrecorded in the formal literature on the rifle. H&R unquestionably built some NATO-caliber rifles in 1955 and 1956. AMF, among others, produced replacement barrels. Beretta rebuilt M1s into .308/7.62 caliber (both remodeling original .30 tubes and producing new ones) and also delivered major quantities built for the shorter cartridge from the very beginning. There are Beretta M1 Garands that bear the BM.59 receiver legend, which indicates that Garands were being ordered and delivered after the Italian NATO rifle had become the Italian standard.

The following is a list of U.S. contract figures and numbers of postwar rifles. Beretta is not included, since, like many European firms, it numbered and coded rifles "to order"—meaning that even if the information were available, which it is not (at least not to me), it would not be particularly meaningful, since there would be many duplicate numbers.

Many of the rifles on later contracts were not produced, or were delivered as match rifles years after the receivers were completed. As a result, the contract figures will have less correlation with the date lists toward their very ends. Also, several collectors have verified that H&R built some small lots of rifles bearing numbers well into Springfield Armory's last batches.

PHOTO 81. The postwar "type 3" rear sight assembly required no tools for adjustment and was locked without need for thumb pressure. These windage knobs are marked with their manufacturer's codes ("SA-WH" for Springfield Armory and "IHC-DRC" for International Harvester), indicating the subcontractor as well.

PHOTO 82. The "type 3" sight assembly gave birth to the fine adjustment 1962-63 National Match rear sight, with its half-minute adjustments, shown here with base and knobs, with standard IHC and SA windage knobs for comparison.

PHOTO 83. Postwar stocks usually carried the "stars 'n' eagle" Defense acceptance stamp, with the exception of some late replacements and the earliest lots from Springfield. H&Rs like this one were smaller than Springfield or IHC markings.

PHOTO 84. Postwar operating rods were not always uniformly marked. Top is an H&R marked "6535382 HRA"; in the middle, one marked "6535382 SA"; and on the bottom, one marked "D-6535382IHC." However, the suffixes used on wartime rods are gone.

PHOTO 85. Postwar bolts were numbered "D 6528287," and there were no longer any subtype suffixes. The other numbers are heat-treat lots and/or order numbers. The refined design was less subject to peening and was stronger.

PHOTO 86. German-made "SuS" (Sauer und Sohn) bolt from the postwar period. Note the unusual arrangement of the parts number code "50652-8287" and the fact that the type reads from the opposite end of American-made bolts. In all other respects, these parts meet every specification. The "50" code may refer to an adoption date or to a German code for the Garand. Note also the two proof/inspector's marks at the bolt's rear.

POSTWAR U.S. GARAND PRODUCTION BLOCKS

Though almost none of these rifles saw service in the Korean conflict, some writers refer to these guns as the "Korean War Period" rifles. Save for the first group of rifles from Springfield (noted in the wartime section), none of these guns bore letter-cartouched stocks.

MANUFACTURER	SERIAL NUMBER BLOCK RANGE
Springfield Armory	4,200,001–4,399,999
International Harvester	4,400,000–4,660,000
Harrington and Richardson	4,660,001–4,800,000
Springfield Armory	5,000,001–5,000,500
International Harvester	5,000,501–5,278,245
Springfield Armory	5,278,246–5,488,246
Harrington and Richardson	5,488,247–5,793,847
Springfield Armory	5,793,848–6,034,228
Springfield Armory	6,034,229–6,099,905

NOTE: A very few experimental guns were manufactured in the 4,800,001–5,000,000 range, by various manufacturers. (Also note that in the serial number block ranges given, some numbers were allocated but never actually used.)

The Springfields

PHOTO 87. A shooter bench sights a postwar Springfield M1, the near-black finish of which is evident in this photo.

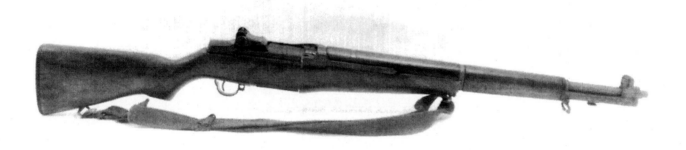

PHOTO 88. A very high-numbered (6,000,000+) postwar Springfield M1 in mint condition.

PHOTO 89. Close-up of postwar Springfield Garand issue barrel, this one dated September 1954 and bearing typical markings, including the postwar part number 65 35448 and several "P" proofs, at least one of which is usually upside down.

PHOTO 90. Close-up of postwar 5,000,000+ rifle with SA-WH marked sights. Note dark finish on metal.

PHOTO 91. The postwar Springfield trigger housing, part-numbered 6528290-SA. There were virtually no changes from the late war units.

The H&Rs

PHOTO 92. Test-firing a very late H&R Garand after restoration.

PHOTO 93. Right-side view of an early H&R Garand.

PHOTO 94. Three match-prepared M1 Garands on H&R receivers. From left: ca. 1964-65 USMC on 5.7 million+ receiver, black-chrome plated; USN "Special Match" from about 1970 and apparently assembled by H&R, with new barrel, serial number range 5.7 million+; and a third, bearing a very early version of the "tin tea cup" nonrotating, hooded National Match sight ca. 1957-58. The rifle on the left was rebuilt at some time and tightly bedded on a World War II cherry replacement stock. All but the center rifle are post-1985 "reimports"—and, no, "imports" is not the correct term for such rifles, unless one is discussing Berettas, which have never been to this country before. The left two are 7.62x51. All three proved to be superb shooters.

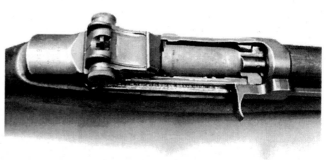

PHOTO 95. Top view of a fairly early H&R, serial #4688464, bearing all original and correct "HRA"-marked parts.

The International Harvesters

PHOTO 96. 1954 "G" series International Harvester, serial #5170972.

PHOTO 97. Early International Harvester receiver serial #4524595.

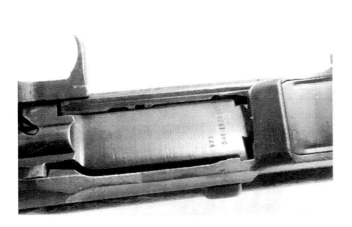

PHOTO 98. Bolt and receiver of a typical IHC rifle.

PHOTO 99. Marking detail of a "D" series International Harvester receiver, showing part number D6528291-D.

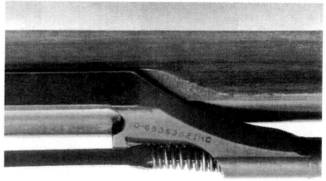

PHOTO 100. Typical "LMR" International Harvester barrel markings, this one dated 7-53. These barrels were also ordered as replacements, and some will carry "HG" or "AFHG" and even "NM" notations. "HG" is for "high grade," "AF" for "air force" (for their competition guns), and of course, "NM" denotes "National Match."

PHOTO 101. International Harvester operating rod data stamping. This rod is fairly early but was located on a very high-numbered rifle on which it was probably original equipment. Most IHC stocks were subcontracted to Overton Mills and will be marked "O" somewhere in the barrel channel.

PHOTO 102. The rare International Harvester "gap letter" serial #4654835 illustrates the unusual letter justification with a large space in the middle, typical of the IHC receivers actually manufactured and completed at Springfield Armory. Note also the heftier contours of these postwar receivers, compared to those in the early wartime section of this book. The thickness of the flat aft of the sight is particularly important.

PHOTO 103. Part number of a "gap letter" International Harvester rifle, noted with heat treat number typical of other Springfield-built rifles, in this case: A 51 D I H C F 6528291. That Springfield actually built these constituted a bailout that should've been a scandal.

The Berettas

The Berettas, photos 104-114 (pp. 107-111) and illustrations (p. 110): Beretta was the last producer of actual military M1 Garands. Delivered at least in the late 1960s and probably well into the 1970s, the Beretta Garands—including many in 7.62x51 NATO—were true, forged M1s from the original postwar configuration.

PHOTO 104.

PHOTO 105. Side view of Beretta M1 Garand, serial #E 1139.

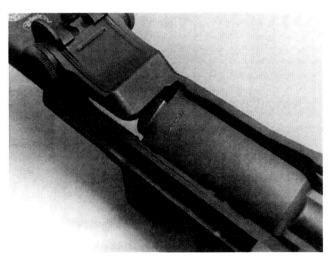

PHOTO 106. Left-side view of an Italian-issue M1 Garand. Note data legend, rear receiver.

PHOTO 107. Bolt top view of Beretta M1 Garand.

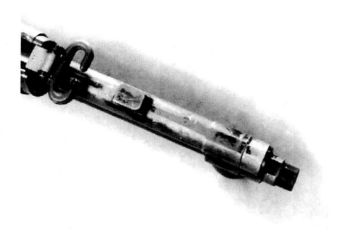

PHOTO 108. "PB" marking emblazoned on the stacking swivel/spacing lug of this M1 Garand was found on a postwar DCM Garand, apparently rebuilt at Beretta or repaired using Beretta parts, probably while on duty in Europe.

PHOTO 109. Rare Allen wrench gas cylinder lock screw by Beretta, ca. 1960 or later.

PHOTO 110. Right view, late Beretta M1 as imported to the United States from Beretta stocks by Springfield Armory, Incorporated (Illinois—not the armory), for the civilian market. This rifle seemed to be unfired and was chambered and marked for 7.62x51mm NATO.

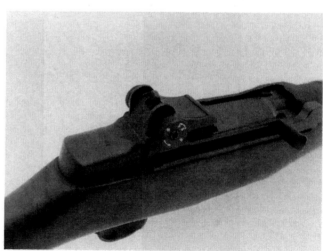

PHOTO 111. 7.62mm NATO Beretta M1, as imported by Springfield, Incorporated sometime after the 1970s. Note the simplified, U.S.-style markings. These were the last true military-specification M1 Garands completed and sold.

PHOTO 112. Very late Beretta M1 Garand receiver, serial #180, apparently off the very last contract. Beretta serial numbers were "to order," and if a country wished to begin its contract numbers at "1," regardless of previous orders, the contract numbers would begin at "1."

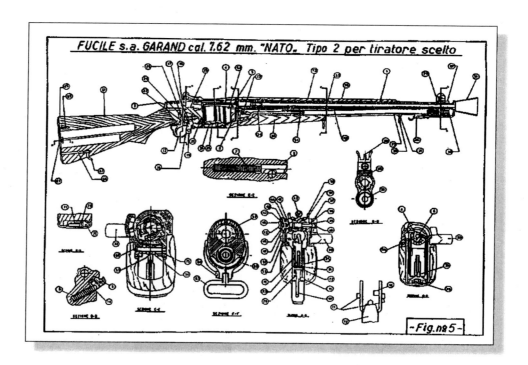

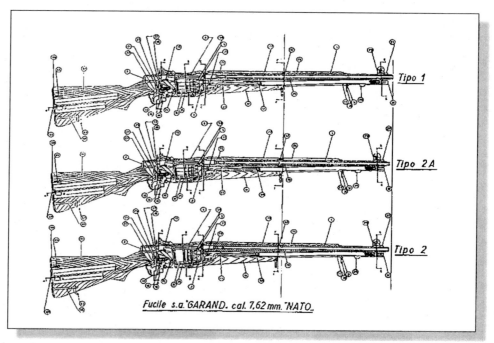

Beretta built and refurbished its own rifles as well as U.S.-built Garands, many of which were reconfigured to its specifications, as in these drawings from official Italian manuals. Tipo 2 per tiratore scelto was basically a standard M1D with a 22-inch reconfigured barrel in 7.62 NATO. Most of these retained 1 in 10-inch twist barrels. Tipo 2 and Tipo 2A were slightly different, shortened 7.62mm rifles of standard infantry configuration. Tipo 1 used new NATO specification 7.62mm barrels with 1 turn in 12 inches right-hand rifling. Most of these rifles remain in Italian service, though in diminishing quantities, mainly in noninfantry units.

PHOTO 113. Lower left view of a Beretta M1 Garand.

PHOTO 114. Arabic markings—most likely Yemeni—on an exported Beretta M1 Garand bespeak the vast and cosmopolitan history of the very last generation of true military M1 Garands.

The Commercial Rifles

M1 Garand Rifle
(With optional sling)

M1 Garand Rifle

NOTE: Outward photographic appearance is
the same for the Standard, National Match
and Ultra Match models.

M1 Garand Rifle
(With commercial mount & scope)

M1-D Garand Sniper Rifle
(Ultra-rare!)
(With M84 mount & scope)

SPRINGFIELD ARMORY, INC.

PHOTO 115. While Fed Ord, Sante Fe Arms, and a few others also produced investment-cast versions of the Garand, it is Springfield Armory, Incorporated's version that is considered the best of the nonmilitary M1 receivers. Serial numbers commenced at 7 million. Early guns from the 1970s used many GI surplus parts; later rifles were virtually entirely produced by Springfield and its subcontractors.

PHOTO 116. The very first commercial Springfield Armory, Incorporated receiver, serial #7,000,000, barreled with an early commercial unit.

SPECIAL-PURPOSE RIFLES AND RARITIES

Special-Purpose Rifles and Rarities, photos 117-124 (pp. 115-119): As soon as the "gas port" rifles became the standard Garands and the system itself was fairly well worked out (about 1941), the armory began to plan for specialized variants and spin-offs. There were long lists of "T" series prototypes, almost all built up and modified from other factory rifles and inherently not available or of interest to collectors except as experiments. The sniper rifles and T26 were never truly "factory" items, but since they were delivered from the armory, the sniper rifles developed there have substantial collector's status. The sniper rifles do not seem to have been selected for accuracy, and the addition of optics simply made aiming at greater distances slightly easier. Since the wartime and immediate postwar scopes were quite poor, most of the M1C and M1D rifles I have shot group better with careful use of the iron sights.

Even the M84—which actually began to see use about 1949–1951—showed poor flatness of field, serious color error, ultracritical eye relief, insufficient power, and bad parallax problems; it would not be acceptable to even a casual shooter. There were better optics available, and one of the mini scandals of the M1 program was the failure to utilize them.

Libby-Owens-Ford, Lyman, and Wollensak made most of the army-issue optics. The M81 and M82 were durable and compact but also suffered from optical problems.

The shooter who can locate a now-discontinued Leupold and Stevens Alaskan of 2 1/2, 4, or 6 power and adapt the C or D mount to the larger optics will find the newer glass a far superior shooting and viewing unit—better sealed and more durable to boot. These employ 7/8-inch tubes like the originals.

The Marine Corps' MC-1 used the Griffin and Howe side mount of the M1C coupled to more modern optics. It is sometimes called the USMC Model of 1952. It uses 1-inch rings and was sometimes found with Leatherwood and other very high-quality scopes affixed. However, these were mainly converted at Marine Corps depots, and little information exists on serial numbers. Therefore, they are difficult to document. They are also very rare, though some, complete with rings but without scopes, were part of Sherwood/Samco's M1 "reimport" shipments from Israel in the mid-1980s. The Marine Corps seems to have bedded many of these rifles. At least one I examined seemed to be fitted with a heavy custom barrel and most of the late National Match fits and adjustments. Stith-Kollmorgen, B&L, and even Unertl optics were apparently sometimes fitted.

The T26 was never really a factory rifle, was never a "Tanker," and was never issued to anyone except for testing purposes (and no, your neighbor's is not the "only" authentic one that actually saw service). The T26 was an AIRBORNE project, and the intention was to replace the M1 carbine—which 'troopers like Gen. James Gavin strongly disliked—with a shorter version of the M1 Garand that paratroopers could deploy fully assembled on drops. The experiment was found to generate excessive recoil and muzzle blast in .30/06 and was brought to its conclusion way too late to see World War II service anyway. The "tanker" monicker is strictly postwar and strictly commercial, and it has absolutely nothing to do with reality.

In .308 or 7.62 NATO, though (especially with a compensator/flash hider attached), the 18-inch-barreled shorty can be a handy rifle and is small enough to carry in the field as a hunting rifle. With a plastic stock, the weight drops an additional two or three pounds. Springfield Armory, Incorporated and Arlington Ordnance market these variants, and they are quite good in .308. However, many of the Fed Ords are downright dangerous, and inspection by a first class armorer is imperative before firing.

Photos and information sketches of the specialized rifles follow.

PHOTO 117. The T26 was a shortened Garand experiment, almost useless in .30/06 but quite handy in .308. This is an Arlington Ordnance rebuild.

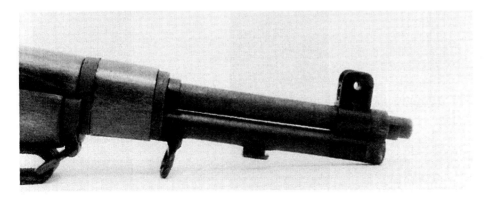

PHOTO 118. The T26 used a shortened operating rod and mechanism, and the front handguard was trimmed to about 2 inches. Many of the substandard Fed Ord rifles deleted the front handguard.

T26

The T26 is a commercial product only but was spun off a series of experiments originated at Springfield Armory and executed mostly at Ft. Bragg and Aberdeen Ordnance Proving Grounds. In the 1944–1946 period, the M1E5 folding stock gun—fairly standard, save for stock and 18-inch barrel—was found to work better when the gas port was enlarged an additional .007 inch. A small batch of the modified rifles in both fixed-stock and folding-stock variants saw fairly extensive testing, and reports were quite negative. Accuracy was also not good using standard ammunition, though loads with faster powders shot quite well.

The operating rod of the T26 is modified, trimmed, and recurved; the follower rod is trimmed to accommodate the thicker spring, which is seated farther back; and, of course, the front handguard is trimmed to just over 2 inches total length.

Lubrication with the 9+ pound rifle is especially important because the compression of all the physical forces on a shorter span increases the overall violence of the action.

M1C

The M1C was spun off the M1E7 project using a Griffin & Howe side scope mount plate, base, and rings, and the original scope was the Lyman M73 "Alaskan." Pins and screws secured this unit to the left side of the receiver, requiring five holes to be drilled into the receiver. By late 1944 the design was standardized, and some saw actual use late in the war. Virtually all standard scopes were nominally 2.5 magnifications, although actual optical measurement of various units proves that they, in reality, were anywhere from just under two power to almost three. Early units bore serial numbers, but it is not correct to say that scopes, mounts, and rifles must all match—especially not on authentic rifles that have seen service. To the collector, a word of caution: there are more fake M1Cs around than real; unless they are very thoroughly documented, buy these as rifles, not as collector's items.

Receiver: all documented units are Springfield Armory, from about 3,000,000 to 3,900,000.

Barrels: originals would be SA units from late 1944 to approximately August 1945, but a replaced barrel of later date would not seriously diminish value.

Base/Mount: Griffin & Howe, stamped with serial number and often other ID numbers.

Optics: M73 Lyman Alaskan or military copy, M81 (crosshairs), M82 (tapered post), M84 a common replacement.

Accessories: flash hiders, cheekpieces, etc.

PHOTO 119. The M84, on its best day, is a lousy scope, but it is compact and durable.

PHOTO 120. Original M84 scopes were far superior to their even weaker predecessors, but are still primitive, dim, and weak by today's standards and suffer from parallax as well. These specimens were reimported to the United States in 1988 and seem never to have been used or refinished.

PHOTO 121. The Leupold & Stevens "Alaskan" series of 7/8-inch tubed scopes, if you're lucky enough to find one, are far better scopes than any of the military units original to the M1C and M1D, though spacers or custom rings are sometimes necessary to fit these larger optics in the correct position.

PHOTO 122. The M1C mount is affixed to the receiver's left. This may be a depot-assembled or "fake" unit, since the alignment pins are absent. The M84 scope is Korean War vintage but was usually retrofitted to earlier rifles still in service. Often, modified 1-inch rings were fitted to allow use of quality optics.

MC-1 (USMC Model of 1952)

MC-1s seem to have been prepared and/or modified to the approximate specification as late as the 1960s. Some others were modified from M1Cs received for USMC service but were found unacceptable.

Most of the later guns incorporated match modifications, and some bore high-quality barrels apparently machined from commercial units at Marine Corps depots.

It is unwise, since there is really no such thing as a "standard" MC-1, to presume anything about a rifle presented as an "authentic USMC" veteran, unless there is some sort of very secure, heavy documentation and verification. And verification does not consist of anecdotes from "buddies" or gun show troopers.

Characteristcs are difficult to specify, but some rifles use the original M1C mount and some use a larger version of same with double levers.

Most common scopes were the "4XD" Stith-Kollmoregen, usually marked MC and serially numbered, but not necessarily to the rifle. Later, Baush and Lomb, Leatherwood, and Unertl optics were often fitted, sometimes with additional support rings added to the middle band area for the long tubes. When this was done and at what level are almost impossible to determine.

I have only seen one MC-1 rifle that was not glass- or epoxy-bedded, and I have seen several in 7.62 NATO, with AMF or H&R barrels. These are usually very accurate rifles and are the only "sniper" versions of the M1 that are really very useful for actual sharpshooting.

M1D

The M1D was too late for World War II, though the M1E8 developmental prototype was tested and the detail design worked up as early as 1944. Most authentic M1D receivers are of World War II vintage, but there seems to have been some armory or depot conversion of later rifles as well. The scope mounting block on the M1D is on the barrel, which requires shortening the handguard. For shooters who merely wish to scope an M1, either this modified barrel (now available new from several suppliers) or the B-Square mount are best for the rifle's long-term value because nothing of interest to collectors needs to be modified to secure the optics. All armory conversions to M1D specifications seem to have been done in the 1951–1953 period, and all authentic M1D barrels apparently came from Springfield Armories. There are no specific serial number ranges for M1Ds, though it is almost impossible that any M1 numbered over 4,500,000 or so could have been converted at the armory. These rifles were not selected for accuracy, and, again, because of the optical limitations of the most common glasses of the period, one is strongly advised not to expect much.

Scopes: M81 or M82, usually M84. A very few M1D rifles have been reimported with a 1-inch ring set, and I have seen one—which must've lived outside the United States for quite some time—with 30 mm rings.

Accessories: cheekpiece, flash hiders, as per M1C.

Note: Most M1Ds seem to have been refinished when converted.

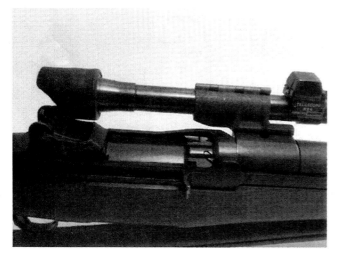

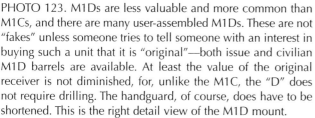

PHOTO 123. M1Ds are less valuable and more common than M1Cs, and there are many user-assembled M1Ds. These are not "fakes" unless someone tries to tell someone with an interest in buying such a unit that it is "original"—both issue and civilian M1D barrels are available. At least the value of the original receiver is not diminished, for, unlike the M1C, the "D" does not require drilling. The handguard, of course, does have to be shortened. This is the right detail view of the M1D mount.

PHOTO 124. M1D Left view of a proven, authentic M1D.

SPIN-OFFS AND DERIVATIVES OF THE M1 GARAND

The Garand was an extremely successful battle rifle, but once the soldiers and engineers and designers saw what they had, they sought to increase its magazine capacity and introduce a selective-fire version and even a squad support version.

The Beretta BM.59 used M1 technology and design directly. In fact, M1s were used to produce BM.59 rifles by remachining the receivers to accept a stripper clip and longer magazine. The American M14 used the receiver and sight design directly, but the receiver was about 1/2 inch shorter and not as strong. Yet the M14 lives on today, both as a small number of GI rifles released to civilians and as a commercial product—such as the Chinese M14 featured in Photo 126, the Smith-forged M14 semiautomatic pictured in top and bottom views compared to a Garand receiver in side aspect, and various cast versions from Springfield Armory, Inc. (its M1A), Fed Ord, and others. M14 could never do for the military what was required—i.e., provide usable automatic fire in the field—but it's an excellent precision high-powered target rifle and is light enough to be carried in the field, with a legal 5-round magazine, for hunting.

Everything that went wrong with the M14 happened because of the compromises made to lighten the weapon while endowing it with automatic capability at too high a rate.

The BM.59, though—which is essentially an M1, modified to accept new doo-dads—uses a shorter, heavier barrel and held up better and could shoot more accurately in full automatic mode. Many, however, were made and issued in semiautomatic only.

Neither of these arms is part of the main M1 story, but they are the denouement of that long-running epic. Failing to explain their ancestry in this work would be a serious omission.

BM59 Nigerian Mark IV Rifle

SPRINGFIELD ARMORY, INC.

PHOTO 125. The BM.59 used the M1 receiver directly, remachined, to produce both selective-fire and semiautomatic rifles for the Italian army and for export. This is the Nigerian service version, delivered from Italy in the late 1960s.

PHOTO 126. The author fires a Smith heat-treated and match-prepared Chinese M14 ca. 1988. This is an all-forged rifle and, once the metallurgy has been brought to specification, is one of the very best M14 clones.

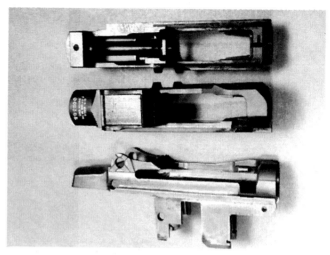

PHOTO 127. The production similarity between the M14 receiver (top two, shown in top and bottom aspects) and the earlier M1 Garand (bottom, side view) is most striking. These forged M14s, by Smith/Western Ordnance, are accuracy lugged, which helps make up for the loss of lug/strut area with the lighter M14 receiver and makes the action more stable in its stock.

PHOTO 128. The M14E2—this one is a Springfield Armory-cast pre-1986 selective-fire clone—was a passable but too-late attempt to make the M14 into a credible selective-fire support weapon.

PHOTO 129. A Smith-built M14 semiauto in match/sniper configuration with scope and cheekpiece, is also a credible hunting rifle.

PHOTO 130. There are civilian-owned and -operated M14s. This one is a TRW-built National Match, long since rendered incapable of fully automatic fire.

YOUR GARAND
AND THE GARAND
OF TOMORROW

PARTS COMPENDIUM—SPECIAL NOTES TO COLLECTORS

The world of firearms seems to be, even more so than the used car profession, the inheritor of the old horse trading tradition. Most of the pure scam artists frequent gun shows, dispensing profitable but erroneous hogwash; luckily, a lot of very good people also hang around gun shows.

Thing is, the flim-flam man will tell you anything to make a profit. The following are some good rules of thumb to keep from getting taken:

1. If a vendor won't allow you to take an M1 out of its stock, don't even consider buying it. It's okay if he wants to be secretive or protective about a Raven or a Jennings, but for what is being asked for Garands these days, if you can't examine the parts, just presume they aren't there. The one exception may be a tightly bedded match rifle, but even then, be suspicious.

2. Never believe anything that can't be documented or verified with printed information from genuine authorities.

3. With parts—especially high-dollar parts—remember that there are actual fakers out there making bogus goodies in huge quantities.

This section deals with some unusual or high-value parts. It is intended to give you a good idea what some things look like. I've included at least one fake in the hope that you can spot it when you see it, which you will. Ironically, most of the bogus parts I've seen are of very high quality, but they're being sold at collector's prices.

Of the thousands of Garands I've seen at gun shows—every single one of which the guy behind the table assured me was "all original, all authentic"—the ones that were, literally, "all original" were those being sold by vendors I mention here. Some of those walking up and down the aisles were all original and authentic, but not all of those, either . . .

Not too long ago, at a gun show in Mesa, Arizona, a man was walking around the building with an M1 that actually had some rather nice parts on it—at least one from more or less every maker who made anything for the rifle. It was, however, badly worn and shot out. It did have old DCM paperwork. His tag read: "All original! Steal at $ 600.00!" I might've offered him $200 for it, mainly for use as a parts source, and because it had a fairly nice World War II cartouched stock. Junk's junk, no matter what the source.

PHOTO 131. Very early "first model" sights, on the windage side, used bright-polished flush nuts. These assemblies were among the many features on the early M1 that had to be replaced quickly. Not only did they shoot loose, but a special tool was required to loosen and/or tighten the windage adjustment. Once it was loosened, the elevation eventually came loose as well.

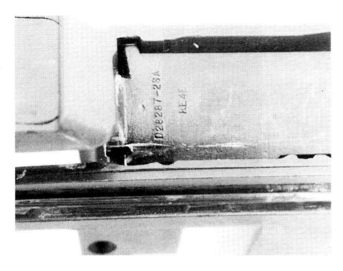

PHOTO 132. This is standard configuration and nomenclature for early bolts, commencing with D28287 and, in this case, a -2 suffix. The dimple is a hardness test trace. Last line is steel supplier, in this case Republic.

PHOTO 133. On the first 100,000 or so Springfield Garands and the first few thousand Winchesters, the milled, grooved variety bands were utilized as standard.

PHOTO 134. Early Springfield barrels such as the 9-40 unit on the bottom—one of the earliest production gas port specimens—placed the part number atop the barrel and the date and manufacturer "upside down" on the barrel's right. Top barrel is a 1943 specimen, for comparison.

PHOTO 135. Earliest followers, such as the bottom unit here, ca. 1937–1939, were quite different from the standardized unit of about 1942 and afterward (top).

PHOTO 136. The rifle shown is one of many examined that combine all original Springfield parts ca. 1943–1944 but are fitted with Winchester barrels of about the same vintage. While one must conclude that these are some kind of field repair, there is a possibility—since this seems so common—that some of Winchester's barrels were fitted to Springfield rifles at the armory for at least a short period.

PHOTO 137. The indicating arrows on Winchester sight drums are referred to as "open," whereas Springfields like this one use "closed" arrows or, as I prefer, "triangles."

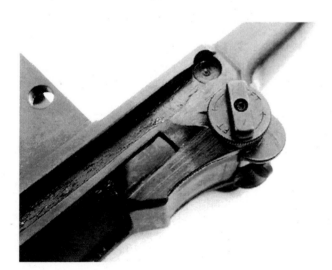

PHOTO 138. These are the "open" arrows of a Winchester windage knob.

PHOTO 139. After about 40,000, the nuts on the short pinion sights were finished—sometimes in a gloss blue, sometimes in phosphate. This rifle had likely been refinished at least once, is likely a rebuild ca. 1940 and probably also about 1946, but has been carefully restored to approximate a conversion ca. late 1940–late 1941 to "gas port" configuration.

PHOTO 140. Rare first model Winchester follower, ca. 1941.

PHOTO 141. All Winchester and very early Springfield hammers are bulkier, carry their part numbers on the side, and, until 1941 or so, carried an extra lube/access hole. This is a -1 Springfield. The excessive bulk had disappeared from Springfield's production by -5.

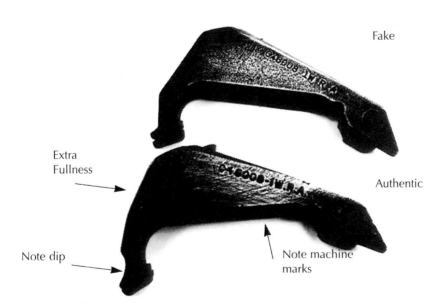

Fake

Extra
Fullness

Authentic

Note dip

Note machine
marks

PHOTO 142. While this photo is a fairly good profile of the late M1 Garand/M14 hammer, with the upper unit being identical to a high-quality, late Garand hammer, its purpose here is not to illustrate the difference in profiles. The lower unit is an authentic Winchester, obvious by the heavy machine marks and "plump" overall configuration. Marked identically, the upper unit is a very nice, actually superior hammer, made very recently, but marked with a duplicate of the Winchester markings of the 1941–1945 period. To a shooter, at a fair price, the fake is fine, but it is definitely not an M1 "original" part and has no collector's value at all. Some collectors suspect these were made in China. One armorer of my acquaintance says they are Taiwanese M14 hammers, remarked.

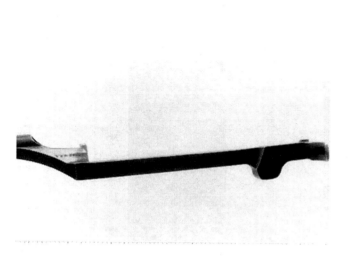

PHOTO 143. Unmodified, unrefinished operating rod from an early Winchester. Note black finish, heavy wear pattern.

PHOTO 144. Topside markings of an original midwar Winchester M1 Garand barrel. Note index mark.

PHOTO 145. Very early Springfield bullet guides bore number and maker designators, and were all milled. This is B8875-1SA from about 1939–1940.

PHOTO 146. Like the later International Harvesters, Winchester front sights were out of specification, spread wider, or, if you prefer, more "bent" than all other manufacturers.

PHOTO 147. Very early Springfield and some early Winchester rear sight spring covers either had no depression groove or carried only a small dimple but were found not to hold securely and to wear excessively.

PHOTO 148. Early short fork follower rods. The bottom one—spring still in place—carries an "A" mark, typical of Winchesters. I have seen these marks on either side and both sides up. These early follow rods were milled, used no rivets, and were serrated. They were replaced because they tended to jump off the mechanism when used with grenade launchers. This type is authentic only to about mid-1942; later at Winchester.

PHOTO 149. C 46025-3 was the last run of number-marked milled trigger guards from the armory, passing out of use by about late 1941 to early 1942. By late 1943, the superior, spring steel stamped units were standard—except at Winchester, which made the change only with its last lot of WIN-13 rifles.

PHOTO 150. Early "arched" lower band, on the lower rifle, ca. early 1943, compared to the late war/postwar "flat" version of the same part.

PHOTO 151. Many Winchester bullet guides are marked "A", sometimes "CM", and they are generally black. Some Springfields also carry the "A" subcontractor mark and are often quite dark. The lighter gray unit here, for comparison, is a later stamped unit.

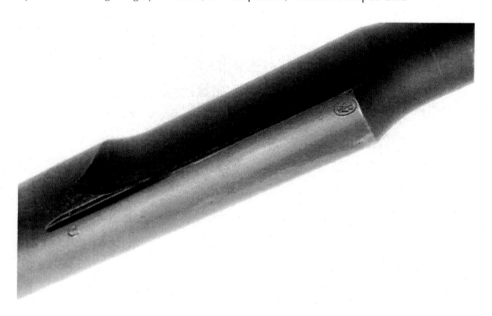

PHOTO 152. "WP" proof and detail index marks on a midwar Winchester M1 Garand barrel.

NOTE: The Garand buff is sincerely invited to copy and recopy the following data sheet (which will work best if you use a copier set up for two-sided copying and use one sheet for each rifle you inspect). Its purpose is to help you share data, aid in restorations, and evaluate specimens in detail.

This sheet is an adaptation of a similar one formulated by David Frenn and run (also with permission to copy) in the *Garand Collector's Association Newsletter*

Don't be too amazed if, even after reading this book, you find some markings that are a mystery to you.

M1   Garand   Data   Sheet & Property Record

date of acquisition_____   Mfg._____S#_____ Mkgs. notes_____
MISC ACQUISITION DATA_____
Receiver: D#_____Heat Lot#_____Bolt Recess: rd____sq_____two tone___
        revision_____rebuild marks_____finish color_____
    general type: M1C__M1D__MC1___"M1936"____NM____Civ Match_____custom_____
    USN Mk.2Mod1___Comm. T26 fits_____Other_____
Bolt: D#_____Heat lot: Hole, bottom_____hole, lug_____
    firing pin, round_____std_____mfg/codes/notes_____
BBL: side mkgs:_____   chrome gas port_____ NM____M1D____7.62_____
                _____other mkgs_____bore condition note_____
    TEG READ_____MZL READ or notes_____color/finish_____

SAFETY: D#_____Location #_____sub #_____extra hole_____
    flat edge_____ round edge_____mfg./mks notes:_____

Trigger: D#_____ other mkgs_____Extra hole_____Sear mkg___finish/color:___

Trigger Housing: D#_____Cloverleaf_____Small hole_____ pad:lg___Sm__
        finish/color notes_____mkg_____mfg_____

Trigger Guard: D#_____milled__stamped___ s w/hook____stamped w/o hook_____
        mfg. code_____ concentric rings_____finish/color_____

Hammer: D#_____Location#: face___side____ exta hole___early notches__
finish/color_____mfg_____
Hammer spring guide: ears____sans ears___finish/color_____
Hammer spring housing: finish_____number____contours_____

FRONT SIGHT: D#_____Blade guard span_____screw cap_____SA/HRA___WRA____PB__
    finish/color_____   contactor_____ IHC___NM___
Gas Cylinder: D#_____color/finish notes_____
        platform: narrow___wide_____ sawcut____flat/round ring(circle one)
        flat/tapered leading edge, bayonet lug (circle one) early_____mzl
        code letters_____mzl plg_____
GAS CYL LOCK: D#_____Misc codes_____Round(early)_____flat/humped_____
        top bevel____no bevel____ color/finish_____notes_____
    Gas Cylinder Lock Screw: single slot__double slot(X form)____gas valve___mkg__
        poppet_____other notes, mkgs_____

Follower: D#_____Early_____narrow front_____wide front_____
    slide: short nose_____long nose____finish/color_____mkg_____#_____
Follower Arm: D#_____single bevel_____double bevel_____prick punch___
    contractor/i.d. code_____no bevel_____other mkg___finish/clr_____
Bullet guide: D#/mfg_____milled____stamped_____finish/clr____
    mkg/misc_____   notched_____ notes:_____

FOLLOWER ROD: D#_____MKG_____Fin/color_____mfg_____
        codes/#'s_____short fork rd__flat____ short fork serr____milled___
        long fork riveted_____notes_____ short fork riveted____

Data sheet.

Operating Rod: D#_____ Mfg_____ NM MKG._____Location mks_____
      relief cut mod_____ handle side: flat____curved____ angle cut:slant__
    finish/clr_____piston measurement____condition____   straight__
Op Rod catch: mkg/d#_____mkd on: inside_____outside_____round front__sq front__
    accelerator mark___finish/color____letters, etc._____
Clip Latch: D#_____Contractor mks.& letters:_____ mk'd:outer__inner__
    round front_____square front___ combination_____open rear_____
Op rod spring: round wire__ Keystone___ finish_____
    compensator spring_____ sq. wire_____ finish_____
rear handguard: D#_____op rod clearance cut____M1D____WRA___birch___wal___
    other notes_____
rear handguard band: d#_____grooved_____milled_____stamped__WRA____clr__

----

lower band: d#_____milled/grooved_____arch_____flat_pin_____
stock ferrule: D#_____milled_____stamped w/o hole____sm hole__lg hole__
    no hole_____finish/color/codes/ltr_____
rear swivel: notes and numbers, screws, etc_____
front handguard: D#_____early ferrule_____N#____sharp/flat bottom
    other notes:_____

....

STOCK: walnut__birch__other____mkgs_____appx. mfg. date_____t.g.cut____
    cartouche_____mfg._____(if known) ord. stamp: large__small___P_____
    Def. ACC ST_____Numbers, locations_____
Butt Section: small hole over lg__holes same___mkgs, other____
buttplate: trapdoor___mkgs_____with border__w/o border___
    no trapdoor ___notes/finish/color_____
LOCATIONS AND SKETCHES:

_____
            REAR SIGHT NOTES
wndg knob #_____ elev. knob#_____base:mfg____code mkgs_____
fine chkr_____ fine chkr_____pt#____color/finish_____
knurled_____ knurled____mkgs_____early:_____
lock nut_____ battle range ntd_____late_____
cross bar, tran____ sht pinion_____cvr. mkgs____cvr grooves____
cross bar, std_____ long pinion:_____finish/clr__cvr. prick punch____clr/fin__
T105E1(Type 3)_____ pinion mkg___cond_____location:outside__inside_____
Coarse chkrd_____ coarse chkrd_____condition_____
AP NM___AP WRA · Arrows: open__closed__   with indents__w/o indents____
SA__HRA__PB__IHC__ With bottom grooves__w/o___   Notes: _____
other_____
Notes_____   Notes_____

THE GARAND MARKETPLACE: RESOURCES AND SUPPLIERS

Note: All the firms listed here were in business, and all the contact information was accurate at the time of publication.

*	also sells other parts
**	also smiths and is capable of assembling and tuning rifle to match specification
***	available in various grades and prices
****	also supplies complete M1 Garand rifles
*****	also available in stainless steel

Match Barrels

Douglas Barrels*****
5504 Big Tyler Road
Charleston, WV 25313

Fulton Armory**
8725 Bollman Place #1
Savage, MD 20763

Krieger Barrels, Inc.** *****
N114 W 18697 Clinton Dr.
Germantown, WI 53022

Springfield, Inc.****
420 W. Main St.
Geneseo, IL 61254
(also supplies service grade)

Springfield Sporters, Inc.****
R.D. # 1
Penn Run, PA 15765

Sarco, Incorporated* ****
323 Union St.
Stirling, NJ 07980

**Extra Heavy Leather M.1907 Type
1 1/4-Inch Slings, as Well as
Embossing with Personalized or Service Insignia**

Leslie Tam
3128 Duval St.
Honolulu, HI 96815

———◆•+•◆———

**Surplus Ammunition, Some Parts,
and (Sometimes) M1 Garand Rifles**

Briklee Trading Co.
13351 D Riverside Dr., Ste. 373
Sherman Oaks, CA 91423

Century Arms International
P.O. Box 714
St. Albans, VT 05478
(also supplies PrviPartizan ammo)

Navy Arms, Inc.
689 Bergen Blvd.
Ridgefield, NJ 07657

Paragon Sales and Service
P.O. Box 2022
Joliet, IL 60434

———◆•+•◆———

**High-Quality Refinishing, Other Technical Services,
Some Accessories (Compensators, Cheekpieces, etc.)
for the M1 Garand**

Smith Arms International**
1701 W. 10th St. #14
Tempe, AZ 85281

———◆•+•◆———

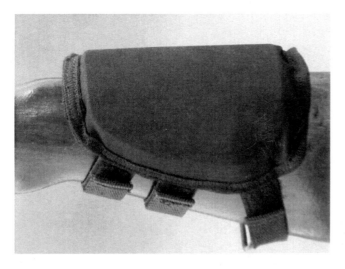

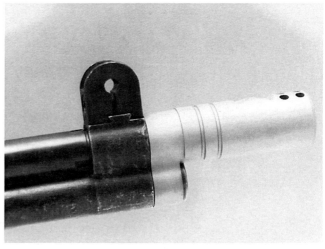

PHOTO 153. Smith's ambidextrous Kevlar/Cordura cheek-piece, designed to service almost any rifle, but especially tailored to the M1 and M14.

PHOTO 154. Smith's M1 Garand compensator, this one hard chromed.

Polymer Stocks for
Garand, M14, and Other Rifles

MPI
5655 NW St.
P.O. Box 83266
Portland, OR 97383-0266

Wood for Stocks and
Handguards for the M1 Garand

Boyd's Gunstock Industries, Inc.
25376 403rd Avenue
Mitchell, SD 57301

Medesha Firearms, Ltd.
10326 E. Adobe Road
Apache Junction, AZ 85220

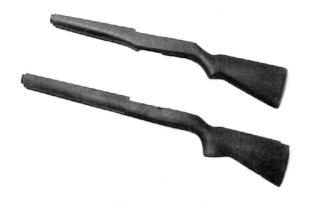

PHOTO 155. MPI fiberglass stocks, on top for the M1 Garand, below for the M14.

PHOTO 156. Bishop's standard format M1 stock of upgraded wood quality.

PHOTO 157. Reinhart Fajen made "heavy match" stocks for the M1 Garand.

PHOTO 158. Complete set of M1 stock and handguards from Fajen, standard grade.

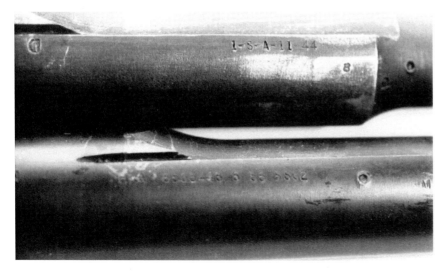

PHOTO 158a. Typical late World War II barrel markings are represented by this 1944 specimen, found on a 2005 Civilian Marksmanship Program rifle, one of the Greek return rifles. Note that there are additional detail markings, including the part number, on top of the barrel.

PHOTO 159. B-Square scope mount atop an M1 bearing BMF/York's straightpull conversion kits.

No-Gunsmithing Scope Mount for the M1 Garand

B-Square Company
P.O. Box 11281
Fort Worth, TX 76110

Straightpull Conversion to Convert M1 to a Bolt-Action Hunting Rifle

Conversions and Kits for Conversions to Allow Use of 20-Round 7.62x51 Magazine on the Rifle

ATP Gun Shop
102 Sarah Ct.
Summerville, SC 29485

Collectors

David H. McClain
1111 Garfield Ave.
Cinnaminson, NJ 08077-2225

Larry Kaufman
Windsor Arms Company
1342 North Cave Creek Road, Suite #1
Phoenix, AZ 85022

(Both are GCA members who were particularly helpful in providing photos and the occasional bit of information. Larry is an FFL dealer with a serious and sincere interest in our favorite old rifle—#100001 is his rifle.)

Historical Association

Garand Collector's Association
P.O. Box 7498
North Kansas City, MO 64116

Primary U.S. Supplier of M1 Garands

Riflesmith

Derrick Martin
Accuracy Speaks Gunsmithing
3960 North Usery Pass Road
Mesa, AZ 85207

(Derrick was also a consultant on many aspects of this book.)

RELOADING FOR THE GARAND AND SIMILAR SEMIAUTOS

Reloading manuals are wonderful—they provide a safety net to the shooter/reloader and trim what could become a lifetime of work to a series of handy notations and intelligent suggestions. The latest Sierra materials, in particular, provide accuracy information based on exhaustive testing of Sierra's splendid line of bullets.

What reloading information seldom does, though, is relate the loads to the operation of automatic recocking systems—that is, high-powered semiautomatics. This means a pet load quite convenient for one's Mauser either won't operate the Garand's action, or it may beat up the gas system and operating rod, eventually leading to excess fatigue and/or breakage.

The loads listed here are designed and "peaked" to the Garand and its spin-offs and variants and are approximately ball equivalent—not necessarily in terms of pressure or velocity, but in terms of gas pressures generated *in the gas system of this family of rifles*.

You'll notice I haven't tabularized the velocity information; this you should test with *your* rifle. These loads were all tested at fairly high and fairly mild temperatures. We did no testing above 110°, none below 4°. With the exception of Hodgdon's VARGET, powders will generate different performances beyond these parameters. And by the way, ammo left in the sun on a hot day very quickly rises well above 110° Farenheit, *so don't do that.*

I specifically caution the reader against the indiscriminate use of either extant formula of 4350 or 4831 and any slower powders in the Garand or other gas-operated semiautos. These powders can work fine, but only at rather low velocity and power levels approximating .30/30.

This phenomenon is due to a coincidence of burn rate, expansion, and temperature in which these powders are hottest right where most rifles bleed off gas. Therefore, they can cause damage if used anywhere near full power.

Optimum bullet velocity windows were explained earlier in "The Practical M1 Garand" and, peripherally, in the historical overview. Another key factor in consistency—which, after all, is all accuracy really is—is a small one: the "pack" of the powder.

The arrangement of air space from shot to shot is always going to be more or less random—influenced by recoil, the violence of the action itself, position of rounds in the magazine or clip, and so on. But a powder that keeps the air space inside the round to a minimum will at least assure that the small influence of air space on burn and expansion rate is further diminished.

The following are some other tips that can contribute to accuracy with almost any rifle, but which are especially applicable to the Garand:

1. Find a way to either buy brass all of the same brand or, better yet, use brass finish, color codings, headstamps, and so on to "code" your loads. I try, for example, to keep all my .308 and .30/06 loads segregated in such a manner that I *know* any nickel-plated brass contains midrange match loads. I use Remington or Federal nickel-plated hulls.

   I start *all* service loads on virgin Winchester primed brass. Heavy bullet loads—that is, long range ammo—is in Remington's conventional brass. Most of my experiments are done on GI hulls. There is no magic to my pattern. When doing "hot" loads or "gentle" stuff, I use nail polish of odd colors to code the cartridges either around the primer or in the extractor groove.

2. Within the above parameters, be sure each lot is fired the same number of times, trimmed identically, and handled the same. And you'll probably want to weigh the brass for ultra-precision loads. Remember, sensible handloaders use far more precise controls than any factory could afford to—not because it's cheaper (though it often is) but because the product works better. If it doesn't work better, you haven't read enough.

3. Extremely heavy and extremely light bullets require careful workup in the Garand and its derivatives. Light bullets (140 grains or less) require hefty powder supplies. Heavy bullets can beat up the guns, and my preference is to work very slowly with anything over 180 grains so as to develop just enough power to operate the rifle. There are very special procedures (talk to your armorer/smith) for potent, long-range loads, and there are some risks involved. But heavy match bullet loads are not available in factory fodder, so this is not an area where "off-the-shelf" is an option.

Lately, I have used ball powders almost exclusively for any shooting that requires a lot of ammo quantity. BLC (2), 748, 760, H380 and some others measure very reliably and generate minimal fouling.

4064 and Hodgdon's new VARGET have lately become favorites for ultra-precison loads.

I use some Winchester primers, but I like CCI's "Benchrest" series for extruded powders and Federal's 210GM Gold Match for ball powders in both .308 and .30/06.

Remington and CCI primers are relatively low pressure and must be used in their "Magnum" versions with ball powders. Federal and Winchester primers generate higher pressures and will work with ball or extruded powders.

The loads listed here should work fine in first quality commercial brass or military brass, though the thicker case walls of GI fodder produce slightly higher pressures.

NOTE: LOADS LISTED HERE ARE NOT IN ORDER OF BURN RATE OR RECOMMENDATION

NOTE: 7.62x51mm NATO and .308 Winchester loads are functionally, but not dimensionally, identical. The most important distinction is in case *capacity*, and where the notations on these loadings specify one type of brass, military or commercial, *only* that type should be used.

147- to 150-gr. Military Ball or Boattail Hollowpoint Bullets, Various Types

WW 748	45.5 gr.
IMR 3031	40.0 gr.
IMR 4895	43.0 gr.
H 4895	41.6 gr.
BLC (2)	46.0 gr.
IMR 4064	44.0 gr. (VARGET very similar)
RE 12	44.6 gr.
RE 15	45.7 gr.
IMR 4064	41.6 gr. *
AA 2495BR	43.4 gr.
Viht N140	43.5 gr.
H335	45.1 gr.

*Special accuracy load, from Sierra, for 150-grain BTHP for use **with commercial brass only.**

168-gr. Match BTHP, Various Manufacturers

WW 748	43.0 gr.
IMR 3031	39.4 gr.
IMR 4895	40.5 gr
H4895	40.1 gr.
IMR 4064	41.4 gr. * VARGET very similar.
RE 12	42.3 gr.
H335	43.5 gr.
BLC (2)	42.9 gr.
Viht N550	45.0 gr.
Viht N150	43.0 gr.
AA-2495 BR	41.5 gr.

*Sierra accuracy load recommendation.
SPECIAL NOTE: 175-grain BTHP bullets *begin* load calculations at about 10 to 12 percent below 168-grain figures. Consult an up-to-date manual for specific recommendations for both calibers with the new 175-grain match bullets.

.30/06/U.S. Caliber .30 Loads

NOTE: If you're using military brass, except for the recent "virgin" .30 being offered by Gibbs and others, it is now quite old. Read the appropriate reloading manuals and check carefully for signs of fatigue. Case capacity is not as radically different in military and civilian brass in this loading but is still significant where mentioned in this text. All loads here, save as noted, were worked up in Federal's nickel-plated "MUP" brass, which is of very uniform volume and weight and is highly recommended by everyone who has used it.

147- to 150-gr. Military Ball of Boattail Hollowpoint Bullets, Various Types

WW 760	53.2 gr. *	H4895	46.0 gr.
WW 748	50.2 gr.	H322	44.0 gr.
AA 2460	46.1 gr.	RE 15	47.8 gr.
VARGET	47.8 gr.	Viht N150	48.5 gr.
IMR 4320	47.6 gr.	IMR 3031	47.6 gr
BLC (2)	47.7 gr.	AA 2460	46.0 gr.
IMR 4064	51.2 gr. **	IMR 4895	48.0 gr.

* Approximately 2640 fps; do not exceed in M1
**Special accuracy load from Sierra, for 150-gr. BTHPs, in commercial brass only. VARGET very similar.

168-gr. BTBP Loads for Precision Shooting, Various Brands

IMR 3031	44.2 gr.	VARGET	45.1 gr.
IMR 4895	44.2 gr.	IMR 4064	45.9 gr. *
RE 19	53.2 gr.	Viht N150	45.7 gr.
RE 15	44.2 gr.	AA 2460	42.8 gr.
H 4895	44.0 gr.	BLC (2)	44.2 gr. **
H 322	43.4 gr.	WW 760	50.2 gr ***
H 335	43.1 gr.	WW 748	46.8 gr.

*Special accuracy load from Sierra. Calculated in MUP brass.
** Loaded in military brass, very clean load.
*** Reduced velocity, good accuracy.

GENERAL NOTES: This load chart is very conservative, but *as always,* the information here was *not* calculated with your rifle and your barrel. Two keys to safe, sane, and accurate reloading are as follows: 1) Have two sources for *all* loads, and 2) use the safe, conservative approach on all data.

These loads were worked up using Federal's 210GM primer.

160. The ball powders can work brilliantly in both M1 calibers. They measure consistently, and they burn cleanly and uniformly.

161. Federal's "MUP" nickel-plated brass is among the most uniform available. It's shown here with Federal's original .30/06M match ammo, some of the best loaded rounds on the market.

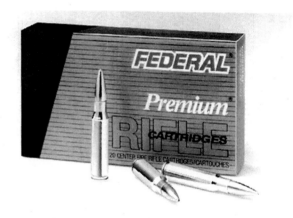

162. Federal's match ammo is now called "Gold Match" and is in its "Premium" line. There is very little factory ammo that can equal these loads, shown here in .308. Only the very best loading discipline, with the best components and controls, can exceed the "GM" in accuracy, and even then, not by much. These loads all feature Sierra's 168-grain Matchking bullet.

SOURCES

Perhaps the most useful publication for the Garand buff who wishes to immerse himself in this legendary firearm is the *GCA Newsletter*, from the Garand Collector's Association, the address of which is listed on p. 141.

For the purist collector, nothing can equal Scott A. Duff's two-volume set on the old rifle: *The M1 Garand of World War Two* and *The M1 Garand: Post World War Two.*

The following two are inexpensive items, primarily useful for the shooter:

Rifle, National Matches. United States Army Weapons & Munitions Command, 1963. (Usually about $4.95.)

The M1 Rifle. National Rifle Association Publications, Washington, D.C. revised in 1985. ($3.95).

The books listed below demonstrate and explain the Garand and the principles behind the rifle. There are other publications with better technical illustrations, but these two contain a lot of information for a reasonable price. They are somewhat dated, and there are some research errors (easily corrected by referral to GCA publications).

Book of the Garand, Maj. Gen. Julian S. Hatcher. Infantry Journal Press, Washington, D.C. Updated in 1977.

Know Your M1 Garand, E.J. Hoffschmidt. Blacksmith Publishers, Chino Valley, AZ. 1975.

Many retired armorers retain copies of various War Department/Department of Defense Technical Operations Orders and manuals that pertain to specific parts and procedure. These are worth copying.